T0038230

FAA-S-ACS-29
Includes FAA-G-ACS-2

U.S. Department of Transportation
Federal Aviation Administration

Airman Certification Standards

Flight Instructor

Helicopter

AVIATION SUPPLIES & ACADEMICS, INC.
NEWCASTLE, WASHINGTON

Flight Instructor Helicopter Airman Certification Standards

Aviation Supplies & Academics, Inc.
7005 132nd Place SE
Newcastle, Washington 98059
asa@asa2fly.com | 425-235-1500 | asa2fly.com

Visit asa2fly.com/acsupdates for FAA revisions affecting this title.

None of the material in this book supersedes any operational documents or procedures issued by the Federal Aviation Administration.

ASA-ACS-29
ISBN 978-1-64425-477-6

Additional formats available:
eBook EPUB   ISBN 978-1-64425-478-3
eBook PDF   ISBN 978-1-64425-479-0

Printed in the United States of America

2028 2027 2026 2025 2024   9 8 7 6 5 4 3 2 1

Contents

U.S. Department
of Transportation

**Federal Aviation
Administration**

Flight Instructor for Rotorcraft Category Helicopter Rating Airman Certification Standards

November 2023

Flight Standards Service
Washington, DC 20591

Foreword

The U.S. Department of Transportation, Federal Aviation Administration (FAA), Office of Safety Standards, Regulatory Support Division, Airman Testing Standards Branch, has published the Flight Instructor for Rotorcraft Category Helicopter Rating Airman Certification Standards (ACS) to communicate the aeronautical knowledge, risk management, and flight proficiency standards for a Flight Instructor Certificate in the Rotorcraft Category Helicopter Rating.

This ACS is available for download, in PDF format, from www.faa.gov.

Comments regarding this ACS may be emailed to acsptsinquiries@faa.gov.

The FAA created FAA-G-ACS-2, Airman Certification Standards Companion Guide for Pilots, to provide guidance considered relevant and useful to the community. The number of appendices in the ACS was reduced and much of the non-regulatory material was moved to the Airman Certification Standards Companion Guide for Pilots. Applicants, instructors, and evaluators should consult this companion guide to familiarize themselves with ACS procedures. FAA-G-ACS-2 is available for download, in PDF format, from www.faa.gov.

Revision History

Document #	Description	Date
FAA-S-8081-7B	Flight Instructor Practical Test Standards for Rotorcraft (Helicopter, Gyroplane)	December 2006
FAA-S-8081-7B	Flight Instructor Practical Test Standards for Rotorcraft (Helicopter, Gyroplane) (with Changes 1, 2, & 3)	July 26, 2016
FAA-S-ACS-29	Flight Instructor for Rotorcraft Category Helicopter Rating Airman Certification Standards	November 2023

Table of Contents

Introduction

Airman Certification Standards Concept

The goal of the airman certification process is to ensure the applicant possesses the knowledge, ability to manage risks, and skill consistent with the privileges of the certificate or rating being exercised, in order to act as pilot-in-command (PIC).

Safe operations in today's National Airspace System (NAS) require the integration of aeronautical knowledge, risk management, and flight proficiency standards. To accomplish these goals, the FAA drew upon the expertise of organizations and individuals across the aviation and training community to develop the ACS. The ACS integrates the elements of knowledge, risk management, and skill required for each airman certificate or rating. It thus forms a more comprehensive standard for what an applicant must know, consider, and do to demonstrate proficiency to pass the tests required for issuance of the applicable airman certificate or rating.

Area of Operation I. Fundamentals of Instructing

Note: *The evaluator must select Task E, Task F, and at least one other Task for initial flight instructor applicants. During a practical test for an added flight instructor rating or flight instructor reinstatement, the evaluator has discretion to evaluate the applicant on Fundamentals of Instructing.*

Task A. Effects of Human Behavior and Communication on the Learning Process

References: *FAA-H-8083-2, FAA-H-8083-9, FAA-H-8083-25*

Objective: To determine the applicant understands human behavior and effective communication, can apply that knowledge, manage associated risks, demonstrate appropriate skills, and provide effective instruction.

Knowledge:	The applicant understands and explains:
FI.I.A.K1	Elements of human behavior, including:
FI.I.A.K1a	a. Definitions of human behavior
FI.I.A.K1b	b. Instructor and learner relationship
FI.I.A.K1c	c. Motivation
FI.I.A.K1d	d. Human needs
FI.I.A.K1e	e. Defense mechanisms
FI.I.A.K2	Learner emotional reactions, including:
FI.I.A.K2a	a. Anxiety and stress
FI.I.A.K2b	b. Impatience
FI.I.A.K2c	c. Worry or lack of interest
FI.I.A.K2d	d. Physical discomfort, illness, fatigue, and dehydration
FI.I.A.K2e	e. Apathy due to inadequate instruction
FI.I.A.K3	Teaching the adult learner.
FI.I.A.K4	Effective communication, including:
FI.I.A.K4a	a. Basic elements of communication
FI.I.A.K4b	b. Barriers to effective communication
FI.I.A.K4c	c. Developing communication skills

Risk Management:	The applicant is able to identify, assess, and mitigate risk associated with:
FI.I.A.R1	Recognizing and accommodating human behavior.
FI.I.A.R2	Barriers to communication.

Skills:	The applicant exhibits the skill to:
FI.I.A.S1	Give examples of how human behavior affects motivation and learning.
FI.I.A.S2	Describe what the instructor can do to deal with:
FI.I.A.S2a	a. Serious abnormal emotional behavior
FI.I.A.S2b	b. Defense mechanisms
FI.I.A.S3	Use effective communication in ground and flight instruction.

Task B. Learning Process

References: FAA-H-8083-2, FAA-H-8083-9, FAA-H-8083-25

Objective: To determine the applicant understands the learning process, can apply that knowledge, manage associated risks, demonstrate appropriate skills, and provide effective instruction.

Knowledge:	The applicant understands and explains:
FI.I.B.K1	Definitions of learning.
FI.I.B.K2	Learning theory as it applies to ground and flight instruction, including:
FI.I.B.K2a	a. Behaviorism
FI.I.B.K2b	b. Cognitive Theory
FI.I.B.K3	Perceptions and insight.
FI.I.B.K4	Acquiring knowledge.
FI.I.B.K5	Laws of learning.
FI.I.B.K6	Domains of learning, including:
FI.I.B.K6a	a. Cognitive
FI.I.B.K6b	b. Affective
FI.I.B.K6c	c. Psychomotor
FI.I.B.K7	Characteristics of learning.
FI.I.B.K8	Scenario-based training (SBT).
FI.I.B.K9	Acquiring skill knowledge, including:
FI.I.B.K9a	a. Stages
FI.I.B.K9b	b. Knowledge of results
FI.I.B.K9c	c. How to develop skills
FI.I.B.K9d	d. Learning plateaus
FI.I.B.K10	Types of practice.
FI.I.B.K11	Evaluation versus critique.
FI.I.B.K12	Distractions, interruptions, fixation, and inattention.
FI.I.B.K13	Errors.
FI.I.B.K14	Memory, including:
FI.I.B.K14a	a. Sensory
FI.I.B.K14b	b. Short-Term Memory (STM) and Long-Term Memory (LTM)
FI.I.B.K14c	c. How usage affects memory
FI.I.B.K14d	d. Forgetting
FI.I.B.K15	Retention of learning.
FI.I.B.K16	Transfer of learning.

Risk Management:	The applicant is able to identify, assess, and mitigate risk associated with:
FI.I.B.R1	Inadequate or incomplete instruction.

| FI.I.B.R2 | Lack of learner motivation. |
| FI.I.B.R3 | Recognizing and correcting learner errors. |

Skills:	The applicant exhibits the skill to:
FI.I.B.S1	Apply educational theories to ground and flight instruction.
FI.I.B.S2	Recognize and correct conditions that undermine the learning process.
FI.I.B.S3	Plan for and use techniques, including realistic distractions that teach flight students how to manage a workload.

Task C. Course Development, Lesson Plans, and Classroom Training Techniques

References: *FAA-H-8083-2, FAA-H-8083-9, FAA-H-8083-25*

Objective: To determine the applicant understands the teaching process, can apply that knowledge, manage associated risks, demonstrate appropriate skills, and provide effective instruction.

Knowledge:	The applicant understands and explains:
FI.I.C.K1	Teaching, including:
FI.I.C.K1a	a. Process
FI.I.C.K1b	b. Essential skills
FI.I.C.K2	Course of training.
FI.I.C.K3	Preparation of a lesson, including:
FI.I.C.K3a	a. Training objectives and completion standards
FI.I.C.K3b	b. Performance-based objectives
FI.I.C.K3c	c. Importance of Airman Certification Standards (ACS) in aviation training curricula
FI.I.C.K3d	d. Decision-based objectives
FI.I.C.K4	Organization of material.
FI.I.C.K5	Training delivery methods, including:
FI.I.C.K5a	a. Lecture
FI.I.C.K5b	b. Discussion
FI.I.C.K5c	c. Guided discussion
FI.I.C.K5d	d. Cooperative or group learning
FI.I.C.K5e	e. Demonstration-performance
FI.I.C.K5f	f. Drill and practice
FI.I.C.K6	Electronic learning (e-Learning).
FI.I.C.K7	Instructional aids and training technologies, including:
FI.I.C.K7a	a. Characteristics of effective instructional aids
FI.I.C.K7b	b. Reasons for use
FI.I.C.K7c	c. Guidelines for use
FI.I.C.K7d	d. Types

FI.I.C.K8	Integrated flight instruction.
FI.I.C.K9	Problem-based instruction.
FI.I.C.K10	Planning instructional activity, including:
FI.I.C.K10a	a. Blocks of learning
FI.I.C.K10b	b. Training syllabus
FI.I.C.K10c	c. Lesson plans

Risk Management: The applicant is able to identify, assess, and mitigate risk associated with:

FI.I.C.R1	Selection of teaching method.

Skills: The applicant exhibits the skill to:

FI.I.C.S1	Prepare an instructional lesson plan using teaching methods and materials appropriate for Task and learner characteristics, including:
FI.I.C.S1a	a. Aeronautical knowledge ground lesson applicable for a classroom
FI.I.C.S1b	b. Maneuver introduction and ground lesson

Task D. Student Evaluation, Assessment, and Testing

References: FAA-H-8083-2, FAA-H-8083-9, FAA-H-8083-25

Objective: To determine the applicant understands evaluation and testing, can apply that knowledge, manage associated risks, demonstrate appropriate skills, and provide effective instruction.

Knowledge: The applicant understands and explains:

FI.I.D.K1	Purpose and characteristics of effective assessment.
FI.I.D.K2	Traditional assessments.
FI.I.D.K3	Authentic assessments, including:
FI.I.D.K3a	a. Learner-centered assessment
FI.I.D.K3b	b. Maneuver or procedure grades
FI.I.D.K3c	c. Assessing risk management skills
FI.I.D.K4	Choosing an effective assessment method.
FI.I.D.K5	Purposes and types of critiques.
FI.I.D.K6	Oral assessment, including:
FI.I.D.K6a	a. Characteristics of effective questions
FI.I.D.K6b	b. Types of questions to avoid
FI.I.D.K6c	c. Answering learner questions
FI.I.D.K7	Assessment of piloting ability.

Risk Management: The applicant is able to identify, assess, and mitigate risk associated with:

FI.I.D.R1	Delivering an assessment.

Skills:	The applicant exhibits the skill to:

Fl.I.D.S1   Use appropriate methods and techniques to assess learner performance in ground or flight training.

Task E. Elements of Effective Teaching in a Professional Environment

References: *FAA-H-8083-2, FAA-H-8083-9, FAA-H-8083-25*

Objective: To determine the applicant understands effects of instructor behavior on effective teaching, can apply that knowledge, manage associated risks, demonstrate appropriate skills, and provide effective instruction.

Knowledge:	The applicant demonstrates understanding of:

Fl.I.E.K1   Aviation instructor responsibilities, including:

Fl.I.E.K1a   a. Helping learners

Fl.I.E.K1b   b. Providing adequate instruction

Fl.I.E.K1c   c. Training to established standards of performance

Fl.I.E.K1d   d. Emphasizing the positive

Fl.I.E.K1e   e. Minimizing learner frustrations

Fl.I.E.K2   Flight instructor responsibilities, including supervision and surveillance during training.

Fl.I.E.K3   Flight instructor qualifications and professionalism.

Fl.I.E.K4   Professional development.

Fl.I.E.K5   Instructor ethics and conduct.

Risk Management:	The applicant is able to identify, assess, and mitigate risk associated with:

Fl.I.E.R1   Fulfilling instructor responsibilities.

Fl.I.E.R2   Exhibiting professionalism.

Skills:	The applicant exhibits the skill to:

Fl.I.E.S1   Deliver ground or flight instruction on an evaluator-assigned Task in a manner consistent with instructor responsibilities and professional characteristics as stated in K1 through K5.

Task F. Elements of Effective Teaching that Include Risk Management and Accident Prevention

References: *FAA-H-8083-2, FAA-H-8083-9, FAA-H-8083-25*

Objective: To determine the applicant understands teaching practical risk management, can apply that knowledge, manage associated risks, demonstrate appropriate skills, and provide effective instruction.

Knowledge:	The applicant understands and explains:

Fl.I.F.K1   Teaching risk identification, assessment, and mitigation.

Fl.I.F.K2   Teaching risk management tools, including:

Fl.I.F.K2a	a. Pilot/Aircraft/enVironment/External Pressures (PAVE) checklist
Fl.I.F.K2b	b. Flight Risk Assessment Tools (FRATs)
Fl.I.F.K3	When and how to introduce risk management.
Fl.I.F.K4	Risk management teaching techniques by phase of instruction.
Fl.I.F.K5	Managing risk during flight instruction, including:
Fl.I.F.K5a	a. Common flight instruction risks
Fl.I.F.K5b	b. Best practices
Fl.I.F.K5c	c. Special considerations while teaching takeoffs and landings
Fl.I.F.K6	Aeronautical Decision-Making (ADM) to include using Crew Resource Management (CRM) or Single-Pilot Resource Management (SRM), as appropriate.

Risk Management: The applicant is able to identify, assess, and mitigate risk associated with:

Fl.I.F.R1	Hazards associated with providing flight instruction.
Fl.I.F.R2	Obstacles to maintaining situational awareness during flight instruction.
Fl.I.F.R3	Recognizing and managing hazards arising from human behavior, including hazardous attitudes.

Skills: The applicant exhibits the skill to:

Fl.I.F.S1	Use scenario-based training (SBT) to demonstrate, teach, and assess risk management and Aeronautical Decision-Making (ADM) skills in the context of a Task specified by the evaluator.
Fl.I.F.S2	Identify, assess, and mitigate risks commonly associated with flight instruction by maintaining:
Fl.I.F.S2a	a. Awareness and oversight of the learner's actions, with timely and appropriate supervision, intervention, or mitigation as needed
Fl.I.F.S2b	b. Awareness of the learner's cognitive/physiological state, with timely action to mitigate anxiety, fatigue, or other obstruction to learning
Fl.I.F.S2c	c. Overall situational awareness of the aircraft's dynamic state, its position in space, and vigilance for unexpected events or changing circumstances that occur in the environment
Fl.I.F.S3	Model and teach safety practices, including maintaining:
Fl.I.F.S3a	a. Collision avoidance while simultaneously providing instruction
Fl.I.F.S3b	b. Avoidance of unnecessary distractions
Fl.I.F.S3c	c. Coordinated flight
Fl.I.F.S3d	d. Awareness of who is manipulating controls through positive exchange of flight controls
Fl.I.F.S3e	e. Continuous awareness of the aircraft's dynamic state and position in the NAS

Area of Operation II. Technical Subject Areas

Note: *The evaluator must select Tasks C and L from this area of operation and at least one other Task.*

Task A. Human Factors

References: *AIM; FAA-H-8083-2, FAA-H-8083-4, FAA-H-8083-9, FAA-H-8083-21, FAA-H-8083-25*

Objective: To determine the applicant understands personal health, flight physiology, aeromedical and human factors, can apply that knowledge, manage associated risks, demonstrate appropriate skills, and provide effective instruction.

Knowledge:	The applicant demonstrates instructional knowledge by describing and explaining:
HI.II.A.K1	Symptoms, recognition, causes, effects, and corrective actions associated with aeromedical and physiological issues, including:
HI.II.A.K1a	a. Hypoxia
HI.II.A.K1b	b. Hyperventilation
HI.II.A.K1c	c. Middle ear and sinus problems
HI.II.A.K1d	d. Spatial disorientation
HI.II.A.K1e	e. Motion sickness
HI.II.A.K1f	f. Carbon monoxide poisoning
HI.II.A.K1g	g. Stress
HI.II.A.K1h	h. Fatigue
HI.II.A.K1i	i. Dehydration and nutrition
HI.II.A.K1j	j. Hypothermia
HI.II.A.K1k	k. Optical illusions
HI.II.A.K1l	l. Dissolved nitrogen in the bloodstream after scuba dives
HI.II.A.K2	Regulations regarding use of alcohol and drugs.
HI.II.A.K3	Effects of alcohol, drugs, and over-the-counter medications.
HI.II.A.K4	Aeronautical Decision-Making (ADM) to include using Crew Resource Management (CRM) or Single-Pilot Resource Management (SRM), as appropriate.

Risk Management:	The applicant explains and teaches how to identify and manage risk associated with:
HI.II.A.R1	Aeromedical and physiological issues.
HI.II.A.R2	Hazardous attitudes.
HI.II.A.R3	Distractions, task prioritization, loss of situational awareness, or disorientation.
HI.II.A.R4	Confirmation and expectation bias.

Skills:	The applicant demonstrates and simultaneously explains how to:
HI.II.A.S1	Associate the symptoms and effects for at least three of the conditions listed in K1a through K1l with the cause(s) and corrective action(s).
HI.II.A.S2	Perform self-assessment, including fitness for flight and personal minimums, for actual flight or a scenario given by the evaluator.

Task B. Visual Scanning and Collision Avoidance

References: AC 90-48; AIM; FAA-H-8083-2, FAA-H-8083-4, FAA-H-8083-9, FAA-H-8083-21, FAA-H-8083-25

Objective: To determine the applicant understands visual scanning and collision avoidance, can apply that knowledge, manage associated risks, demonstrate pilot-in-command skills, and provide effective instruction.

Knowledge:	The applicant demonstrates instructional knowledge by describing and explaining:
HI.II.B.K1	Environmental conditions that degrade vision.
HI.II.B.K2	Vestibular and visual illusions.
HI.II.B.K3	"See and Avoid" responsibilities.
HI.II.B.K4	Visual scanning procedure and the importance of peripheral vision.
HI.II.B.K5	Aircraft blind spots and clearing procedures.
HI.II.B.K6	Visual cues of an impending mid-air collision.
HI.II.B.K7	Situations that create the greatest collision risk.
HI.II.B.K8	Division of attention inside and outside the aircraft.

Risk Management:	The applicant explains and teaches how to identify and manage risk associated with:
HI.II.B.R1	Distractions to visual scanning.
HI.II.B.R2	Relaxed intermediate focal distance.
HI.II.B.R3	High volume operational environments.
HI.II.B.R4	Collision reaction time.
HI.II.B.R5	Use of a safety pilot.

Skills:	The applicant demonstrates and simultaneously explains how to:
HI.II.B.S1	Effectively scan using short regularly spaced eye movements.
HI.II.B.S2	Scan around physical obstructions.
HI.II.B.S3	Use appropriate visual scanning techniques.
HI.II.B.S4	Use electronic traffic alert systems, if available.

Task C. Runway Incursion Avoidance

References: AC 91-73; AIM; Chart Supplements; FAA-H-8083-2, FAA-H-8083-4, FAA-H-8083-9, FAA-H-8083-21, FAA-H-8083-25

Objective: To determine the applicant understands runway incursion avoidance, can apply that knowledge, manage associated risks, demonstrate appropriate skills, and provide effective instruction.

Knowledge:	The applicant demonstrates instructional knowledge by describing and explaining:
HI.II.C.K1	Runway incursion definition.
HI.II.C.K2	Taxi instructions/clearances.
HI.II.C.K3	The importance of recording taxi instructions and reviewing taxi routes on the airport diagram.

HI.II.C.K4	Airport markings, signs, and lights including the importance of hold lines associated with runways.
HI.II.C.K5	Appropriate flight deck activities during taxiing, including taxi route planning, briefing the location of Hot Spots, communicating and coordinating with ATC.
HI.II.C.K6	Communication and operational procedures at uncontrolled airports.

Risk Management:	The applicant explains and teaches how to identify and manage risk associated with:
HI.II.C.R1	Distractions, task prioritization, loss of situational awareness, or disorientation.
HI.II.C.R2	Confirmation or expectation bias as related to taxi instructions.
HI.II.C.R3	Entering or crossing runways.
HI.II.C.R4	Night taxi operations.
HI.II.C.R5	Low visibility taxi operations.
HI.II.C.R6	Runway incursion after landing.
HI.II.C.R7	Operating on taxiways between parallel runways.

Skills:	The applicant demonstrates how to:
HI.II.C.S1	Deliver instruction on the elements and techniques for runway incursion avoidance.

Task D. Principles of Flight

References: FAA-H-8083-2, FAA-H-8083-4, FAA-H-8083-9, FAA-H-8083-21, FAA-H-8083-25; POH/RFM

Objective: To determine the applicant understands aerodynamics appropriate to the desired instructor certificate, can apply that knowledge, manage associated risks, demonstrate appropriate skills, and provide effective instruction.

Knowledge:	The applicant demonstrates instructional knowledge by describing and explaining:
HI.II.D.K1	Lift, weight, thrust, and drag.
HI.II.D.K2	Airfoils, including terminology, definitions, and types.
HI.II.D.K3	Torque effect and translating tendency.
HI.II.D.K4	Gyroscopic precession.
HI.II.D.K5	Blade flapping and coning.
HI.II.D.K6	Coriolis effect.
HI.II.D.K7	Pendular action.
HI.II.D.K8	Dissymmetry of lift.
HI.II.D.K9	Retreating blade stall.
HI.II.D.K10	Translational lift, including effective translational lift (ETL).
HI.II.D.K11	Transverse flow effect.
HI.II.D.K12	Aerodynamics of autorotative flight.
HI.II.D.K13	Rotor system characteristics.

Risk
Management: The applicant explains and teaches how to identify and manage risk associated with:

HI.II.D.R1	The basic aerodynamic principles of flight.

Skills: The applicant demonstrates and simultaneously explains how to:

HI.II.D.S1	Deliver instruction on principles of flight, including at least three of the elements listed K1 through K13.

Task E. Flight Controls

References: FAA-H-8083-2, FAA-H-8083-4, FAA-H-8083-9, FAA-H-8083-21, FAA-H-8083-25; POH/RFM

Objective: To determine the applicant understands the flight controls on the helicopter provided for the flight test, can apply that knowledge, manage associated risks, demonstrate appropriate skills, and provide effective instruction.

Knowledge: The applicant demonstrates instructional knowledge by describing and explaining:

HI.II.E.K1	Cyclic.
HI.II.E.K2	Collective.
HI.II.E.K3	Antitorque pedals.
HI.II.E.K4	Throttle and governor, if equipped.

Risk
Management: The applicant explains and teaches how to identify and manage risk associated with:

HI.II.E.R1	Use of flight controls.
HI.II.E.R2	Uncoordinated flight.
HI.II.E.R3	Flight control inputs when operating too close to the ground or other obstructions.

Skills: The applicant demonstrates and simultaneously explains how to:

HI.II.E.S1	Operate the flight controls.

Task F. Operation of Systems

References: FAA-H-8083-2, FAA-H-8083-4, FAA-H-8083-9, FAA-H-8083-21, FAA-H-8083-25; POH/RFM

Objective: To determine the applicant understands systems on the helicopter provided for the flight test, can apply that knowledge, manage associated risks, demonstrate appropriate skills, and provide effective instruction.

Note: If K1 is selected, the evaluator assesses the applicant's knowledge of at least three sub-elements.

Knowledge: The applicant demonstrates instructional knowledge by describing and explaining:

HI.II.F.K1	Helicopter systems, including:
HI.II.F.K1a	a. Flight controls, trim, and if installed, stability control
HI.II.F.K1b	b. Powerplant(s)
HI.II.F.K1c	c. Main rotor and antitorque systems
HI.II.F.K1d	d. Transmission and associated drive shafts

HI.II.F.K1e	e. Fuel, oil, and hydraulic
HI.II.F.K1f	f. Landing gear, brakes, steering, skids, or floats, as applicable
HI.II.F.K1g	g. Avionics
HI.II.F.K1h	h. Electrical
HI.II.F.K1i	i. Pitot-static, vacuum/pressure, and associated flight instruments
HI.II.F.K1j	j. Environmental
HI.II.F.K1k	k. Anti-icing and deicing, including carburetor heat, if applicable
HI.II.F.K2	Indications of and procedures for managing system abnormalities or failures.

Risk Management:	The applicant explains and teaches how to identify and manage risk associated with:
HI.II.F.R1	Detection of system malfunctions or failures.
HI.II.F.R2	Management of a system failure.
HI.II.F.R3	Monitoring and management of automated systems.
HI.II.F.R4	Providing instruction in unfamiliar aircraft or operating with unfamiliar flight display systems and avionics.

Skills:	The applicant demonstrates and simultaneously explains how to:
HI.II.F.S1	Operate at least three of the helicopter's systems listed in K1a through K1k.
HI.II.F.S2	Complete the appropriate checklist(s).

Task G. Performance and Limitations

References: FAA-H-8083-2, FAA-H-8083-4, FAA-H-8083-9, FAA-H-8083-21, FAA-H-8083-25; POH/RFM

Objective: To determine the applicant understands helicopter performance and limitations, can apply that knowledge, manage associated risks, demonstrate appropriate skills, and provide effective instruction

Knowledge:	The applicant demonstrates instructional knowledge by describing and explaining:
HI.II.G.K1	Elements related to performance and limitations by explaining the use of charts, tables, and data to determine performance.
HI.II.G.K2	Factors affecting performance, including:
HI.II.G.K2a	a. Atmospheric conditions
HI.II.G.K2b	b. Pilot technique
HI.II.G.K2c	c. Airport, heliport, helipad, or unprepared surface environment
HI.II.G.K2d	d. Loading and weight and balance
HI.II.G.K2e	e. Helicopter configuration
HI.II.G.K3	Weight and balance terms, including: basic empty weight, maximum gross weight, arm, moment, reference datum, center of gravity (CG) and CG limits, and useful load.
HI.II.G.K4	Methods for computing longitudinal/lateral CG.
HI.II.G.K5	Aerodynamics.

| HI.II.G.K6 | Height/Velocity (H/V) diagram according to the Rotorcraft Flight Manual (RFM). |

Risk Management: The applicant explains and teaches how to identify and manage risk associated with:

HI.II.G.R1	Use of performance charts, tables, and data.
HI.II.G.R2	Helicopter limitations.
HI.II.G.R3	Possible differences between calculated performance and actual performance.
HI.II.G.R4	Exceeding weight limits.
HI.II.G.R5	Operating outside of CG limits.
HI.II.G.R6	Shifting, adding, and removing weight.
HI.II.G.R7	Retreating blade stall.
HI.II.G.R8	Situations that lead to loss of tail rotor/antitorque effectiveness (LTE).

Skills: The applicant demonstrates and simultaneously explains how to:

| HI.II.G.S1 | Use appropriate helicopter performance charts, tables, and data. |
| HI.II.G.S2 | Compute the weight and balance, correct out-of-center of gravity loading errors and determine if the weight and balance remains within limits during all phases of flight. |

Task H. National Airspace System

References: *14 CFR parts 71, 91, 93; AIM; FAA-H-8083-2, FAA-H-8083-4, FAA-H-8083-9, FAA-H-8083-21, FAA-H-8083-25; Helicopter Route Charts; VFR Navigation Charts*

Objective: To determine the applicant understands the National Airspace System, can apply that knowledge, manage associated risks, demonstrate appropriate skills, and provide effective instruction.

Knowledge: The applicant demonstrates instructional knowledge by describing and explaining:

HI.II.H.K1	Airspace classes and associated requirements and limitations.
HI.II.H.K2	Chart symbols.
HI.II.H.K3	Special use airspace (SUA), special flight rules areas (SFRA), temporary flight restrictions (TFR), and other airspace areas.
HI.II.H.K4	Currency of publications.
HI.II.H.K5	Special visual flight rules (VFR) requirements.

Risk Management: The applicant explains and teaches how to identify and manage risk associated with:

| HI.II.H.R1 | Various classes and types of airspace. |

Skills: The applicant demonstrates and simultaneously explains how to:

HI.II.H.S1	Identify and comply with the requirements for basic VFR weather minimums and flying in particular classes of airspace.
HI.II.H.S2	Correctly identify airspace and operate in accordance with associated communication and equipment requirements.
HI.II.H.S3	Identify the requirements for operating in SUA or within a TFR. Identify and comply with special air traffic rules (SATR) and SFRA operations, if applicable.

Task I. Navigation Systems and Radar Services

References: AC 91-78; AIM; FAA-H-8083-2, FAA-H-8083-4, FAA-H-8083-9, FAA-H-8083-21, FAA-H-8083-25

Objective: To determine the applicant understands navigation systems and radar services, can apply that knowledge, manage associated risks, demonstrate appropriate skills, and provide effective instruction.

Note: The evaluator should reference the manufacturer's equipment supplement(s) as necessary for appropriate limitations, procedures, etc.

Knowledge:	The applicant demonstrates instructional knowledge by describing and explaining:
HI.II.I.K1	Ground-based navigation (identification, orientation, course determination, equipment, tests, regulations, interference, appropriate use of navigation data, and signal integrity).
HI.II.I.K2	Satellite-based navigation (e.g., equipment, regulations, authorized use of databases, and Receiver Autonomous Integrity Monitoring (RAIM)).
HI.II.I.K3	Radar assistance to visual flight rules (VFR) aircraft (e.g., operations, equipment, available services, traffic advisories).
HI.II.I.K4	Transponder (Mode(s) A, C, and S) and Automatic Dependent Surveillance-Broadcast (ADS-B).

Risk Management:	The applicant explains and teaches how to identify and manage risk associated with:
HI.II.I.R1	Management of automated navigation and autoflight systems.
HI.II.I.R2	Distractions, task prioritization, loss of situational awareness, or disorientation.
HI.II.I.R3	Limitations of the navigation system in use.
HI.II.I.R4	Loss of a navigation signal.
HI.II.I.R5	Use of an electronic flight bag (EFB), if used.

Skills:	The applicant demonstrates and simultaneously explains how to:
HI.II.I.S1	Use an airborne electronic navigation system.
HI.II.I.S2	Determine the aircraft's position using the navigation system.
HI.II.I.S3	Intercept and track a given course, radial, or bearing.
HI.II.I.S4	Recognize and describe the indication of station or waypoint passage.
HI.II.I.S5	Use proper communication procedures when utilizing radar services.

Task J. Navigation and Cross-Country Flight Planning

References: 14 CFR part 91; AC 91.21-1; AIM; Chart Supplements; FAA-H-8083-2, FAA-H-8083-4, FAA-H-8083-9, FAA-H-8083-21, FAA-H-8083-25; Helicopter Route Charts; NOTAMs; POH/RFM; VFR Navigation Charts

Objective: To determine the applicant understands navigation and cross-country flight planning, can apply that knowledge, manage associated risks, demonstrate appropriate skills, and provide effective instruction.

Note: Preparation, presentation, and explanation of a computer-generated flight plan is an acceptable option.

Knowledge:	The applicant demonstrates instructional knowledge by describing and explaining:
HI.II.J.K1	Route planning, including consideration of different classes and special use airspace (SUA) and selection of appropriate and available navigation/communication systems and facilities.
HI.II.J.K2	Altitude selection accounting for terrain and obstacles, autorotation requirements of the helicopter, VFR cruising altitudes, and the effect of wind.
HI.II.J.K3	Plotting a course.
HI.II.J.K4	Power setting selection.
HI.II.J.K5	Calculating:
HI.II.J.K5a	a. Time, climb and descent rates, course, distance, heading, true airspeed, and groundspeed
HI.II.J.K5b	b. Estimated time of arrival, including conversion to universal coordinated time (UTC)
HI.II.J.K5c	c. Fuel requirements, including reserve
HI.II.J.K6	Elements of a VFR flight plan.
HI.II.J.K7	Correlate weather information to make a go/no-go decision.
HI.II.J.K8	Procedures for activating and closing a VFR flight plan.
HI.II.J.K9	Magnetic compass errors.
HI.II.J.K10	Pilotage and dead reckoning.
HI.II.J.K11	Planned calculations versus actual results and required corrections.
HI.II.J.K12	Diversion and lost procedures.
HI.II.J.K13	Inflight intercept procedures.
HI.II.J.K14	Use of an electronic flight bag (EFB), if used.
HI.II.J.K15	Chart symbols.

Risk Management:	The applicant explains and teaches how to identify and manage risk associated with:
HI.II.J.R1	Pilot.
HI.II.J.R2	Aircraft.
HI.II.J.R3	Environment (e.g., weather, airports, airspace, terrain, obstacles, including wire strike hazards).
HI.II.J.R4	External pressures.
HI.II.J.R5	Limitations of air traffic control (ATC) services.
HI.II.J.R6	Fuel planning.

Skills:	The applicant demonstrates and simultaneously explains how to:
HI.II.J.S1	Prepare, present, and explain a cross-country flight plan assigned by the evaluator, including a risk analysis to the first fuel stop.
HI.II.J.S2	Apply pertinent information from appropriate and current aeronautical charts, Chart Supplements; Notices to Air Missions (NOTAMs) relative to airport/heliport/helipad/landing area, runway and taxiway closures; and other flight publications.
HI.II.J.S3	Create a navigation plan and simulate filing a VFR flight plan.
HI.II.J.S4	Recalculate fuel reserves based on a scenario provided by the evaluator.

Task K. 14 CFR and Publications

References: *14 CFR parts 1, 61, 91; 49 CFR part 830; AIM; Chart Supplements; FAA-H-8083-2, FAA-H-8083-4, FAA-H-8083-9, FAA-H-8083-21, FAA-H-8083-25; POH/RFM*

Objective: To determine the applicant understands the Code of Federal Regulations and other relevant publications, can apply that knowledge, manage associated risks, demonstrate appropriate skills, and provide effective instruction.

Knowledge:	The applicant demonstrates instructional knowledge by describing and explaining:
HI.II.K.K1	14 CFR parts 1, 61, and 91.
HI.II.K.K2	49 CFR part 830.
HI.II.K.K3	Advisory Circulars, INFOs, and SAFOs.
HI.II.K.K4	Airman Certification Standards or Practical Test Standards.
HI.II.K.K5	Pilot's Operating Handbooks or flight manuals.
HI.II.K.K6	Aeronautical Information Manual (AIM).

Risk Management:	The applicant explains and teaches how to identify and manage risk associated with:
HI.II.K.R1	Use of expired charts, manuals, or publications without current updates.

Skills:	The applicant demonstrates and simultaneously explains how to:
HI.II.K.S1	Teach at least one of the elements listed in K1 through K6.

Task L. Endorsements and Logbook Entries

References: *14 CFR part 61; AC 61-65; FAA-H-8083-2, FAA-H-8083-4, FAA-H-8083-9, FAA-H-8083-21, FAA-H-8083-25*

Objective: To determine the applicant understands logbook entries and endorsements, can apply that knowledge, manage associated risks, demonstrate appropriate skills, and provide effective instruction.

Knowledge:	The applicant demonstrates instructional knowledge by describing and explaining:
HI.II.L.K1	Required logbook entries for instruction given.
HI.II.L.K2	Required student pilot pre-solo knowledge test, solo endorsements, and logbook entries.
HI.II.L.K3	Other required pilot logbook endorsements (e.g., touchdown autorotation, Special Federal Aviation Regulation (SFAR)).
HI.II.L.K4	Preparation of a recommendation for a pilot practical test, including appropriate logbook entry and relevant certificate/rating application for:
HI.II.L.K4a	a. Initial pilot certification
HI.II.L.K4b	b. Additional pilot certification
HI.II.L.K4c	c. Additional aircraft qualification
HI.II.L.K5	Endorsement of a pilot logbook for the satisfactory completion of an FAA flight review.
HI.II.L.K6	Required flight instructor records.
HI.II.L.K7	Flight instructor renewal and reinstatement requirements.

Risk Management: The applicant is able to identify, assess, and mitigate risk associated with:

HI.II.L.R1	Endorsements without appropriate limitations or expiration dates.

Skills: The applicant demonstrates and simultaneously explains how to:

HI.II.L.S1	Describe and prepare logbook entries/endorsements required for at least two of the events specified in the elements or sub-elements of K1 through K5.

Task M. Night Operations

References: *14 CFR part 91; AIM; FAA-H-8083-2, FAA-H-8083-4, FAA-H-8083-9, FAA-H-8083-21, FAA-H-8083-25; POH/RFM*

Objective: To determine the applicant understands night operations, can apply that knowledge, manage associated risks, demonstrate appropriate skills, and provide effective instruction.

Knowledge: The applicant demonstrates instructional knowledge by describing and explaining:

HI.II.M.K1	Physiological aspects of vision related to night flying.
HI.II.M.K2	Lighting systems identifying airports/heliports/helipads/landing areas, runways, taxiways and obstructions, as well as pilot controlled lighting.
HI.II.M.K3	Helicopter equipment and lighting requirements for night operations.
HI.II.M.K4	Personal equipment essential for night flight.
HI.II.M.K5	Night orientation, navigation, chart reading techniques and methods for maintaining night vision effectiveness.
HI.II.M.K6	Night taxi operations.
HI.II.M.K7	Interpretation of traffic position and direction based solely on position lights.
HI.II.M.K8	Use of instruments to verify the aircraft attitude at night.
HI.II.M.K9	Visual illusions at night.
HI.II.M.K10	Appropriate use of automation, if applicable.

Risk Management: The applicant explains and teaches how to identify and manage risk associated with:

HI.II.M.R1	Inoperative equipment.
HI.II.M.R2	Weather considerations specific to night operations.
HI.II.M.R3	Collision hazards.
HI.II.M.R4	Distractions, task prioritization, loss of situational awareness, or disorientation.
HI.II.M.R5	Effect of visual illusions and night adaptation during all phases of night flying.
HI.II.M.R6	Runway incursion.
HI.II.M.R7	Night currency versus proficiency.

Skills: The applicant demonstrates how to:

HI.II.M.S1	Teach at least one of the elements listed in K1 through K10.

Area of Operation III. Preflight Preparation

Note: *The evaluator must select at least one Task from this Area of Operation.*

Task A. Pilot Qualifications

References: *14 CFR parts 61, 68, 91; AC 60-28, AC 68-1; FAA-H-8083-2, FAA-H-8083-4, FAA-H-8083-9, FAA-H-8083-21, FAA-H-8083-25; POH/RFM*

Objective: To determine the applicant understands pilot training and qualification requirements for different levels of pilot certificate including student pilot, recreational pilot, private pilot, commercial pilot, and flight instructor; can apply that knowledge, manage associated risks, demonstrate appropriate skills, and provide effective instruction.

Knowledge:	The applicant demonstrates instructional knowledge by describing and explaining:
HI.III.A.K1	Certification, currency, and recordkeeping requirements, including training and logbook entries.
HI.III.A.K2	Privileges and limitations of pilot certificates and ratings at student pilot, recreational, private, commercial, and flight instructor levels.
HI.III.A.K3	Medical certificates: class, expiration, privileges, temporary disqualifications, and operations under BasicMed.
HI.III.A.K4	Documents pilots must possess to exercise privileges of the specified certificate(s) and rating(s).

Risk Management:	The applicant explains and teaches how to identify and manage risk associated with:
HI.III.A.R1	Proficiency versus currency.
HI.III.A.R2	Flying an unfamiliar helicopter or operating with unfamiliar flight display systems and avionics.

Skills:	The applicant demonstrates how to:
HI.III.A.S1	Deliver instruction on at least two of the elements specified in K1 through K4.

Task B. Airworthiness Requirements

References: *14 CFR parts 27, 29, 39, 43, 91; FAA-H-8083-2, FAA-H-8083-4, FAA-H-8083-9, FAA-H-8083-21, FAA-H-8083-25*

Objective: To determine the applicant understands airworthiness requirements, including aircraft certificates, can apply that knowledge, manage associated risks, demonstrate appropriate skills, and provide effective instruction.

Knowledge:	The applicant demonstrates instructional knowledge by describing and explaining:
HI.III.B.K1	General airworthiness requirements and compliance for helicopters, including:
HI.III.B.K1a	a. Location and expiration dates of required aircraft certificates
HI.III.B.K1b	b. Required inspections and aircraft logbook documentation
HI.III.B.K1c	c. Airworthiness Directives and Special Airworthiness Information Bulletins
HI.III.B.K1d	d. Purpose and procedure for obtaining a special flight permit
HI.III.B.K2	Pilot-performed preventive maintenance.
HI.III.B.K3	Equipment requirements for day and night VFR flight, including:

HI.III.B.K3a	a. Flying with inoperative equipment
HI.III.B.K3b	b. Using an approved Minimum Equipment List (MEL)
HI.III.B.K3c	c. Kinds of Operation Equipment List (KOEL)
HI.III.B.K3d	d. Required discrepancy records or placards
HI.III.B.K4	Special airworthiness certificate aircraft operating limitations, if applicable.

Risk Management: The applicant explains and teaches how to identify and manage risk associated with:

| HI.III.B.R1 | Inoperative equipment discovered prior to flight. |

Skills: The applicant demonstrates and simultaneously explains how to:

HI.III.B.S1	Locate and describe helicopter airworthiness and registration information.
HI.III.B.S2	Determine the helicopter is airworthy in the scenario given by the evaluator.
HI.III.B.S3	Apply appropriate procedures for operating with inoperative equipment in a scenario given by the evaluator.

Task C. Weather Information

References: *14 CFR part 91; AC 91-92; AIM; FAA-H-8083-2, FAA-H-8083-4, FAA-H-8083-9, FAA-H-8083-21, FAA-H-8083-25, FAA-H-8083-28*

Objective: To determine the applicant understands weather information, can apply that knowledge, manage associated risks, demonstrate appropriate skills, and provide effective instruction.

Note: *If K2 is selected, the evaluator must assess the applicant's knowledge of at least three sub-elements.*

Note: *If K3 is selected, the evaluator must assess the applicant's knowledge of at least three sub-elements.*

Knowledge: The applicant demonstrates instructional knowledge by describing and explaining:

HI.III.C.K1	Sources of weather data (e.g., National Weather Service, Flight Service) for flight planning purposes.
HI.III.C.K2	Acceptable weather products and resources required for preflight planning, current and forecast weather for departure, en route, and arrival phases of flight such as:
HI.III.C.K2a	a. Airport Observations (METAR and SPECI) and Pilot Observations (PIREP)
HI.III.C.K2b	b. Surface Analysis Chart, Ceiling and Visibility Chart (CVA)
HI.III.C.K2c	c. Terminal Aerodrome Forecasts (TAF)
HI.III.C.K2d	d. Graphical Forecasts for Aviation (GFA)
HI.III.C.K2e	e. Wind and Temperature Aloft Forecast (FB)
HI.III.C.K2f	f. Convective Outlook (AC)
HI.III.C.K2g	g. Inflight Aviation Weather Advisories including Airmen's Meteorological Information (AIRMET), Significant Meteorological Information (SIGMET), and Convective SIGMET
HI.III.C.K3	Meteorology applicable to the departure, en route, alternate, and destination under visual flight rules (VFR) in Visual Meteorological Conditions (VMC), including expected climate and hazardous conditions such as:
HI.III.C.K3a	a. Atmospheric composition and stability

HI.III.C.K3b	b. Wind (e.g., windshear, mountain wave, factors affecting wind, etc.)
HI.III.C.K3c	c. Temperature and heat exchange
HI.III.C.K3d	d. Moisture/precipitation
HI.III.C.K3e	e. Weather system formation, including air masses and fronts
HI.III.C.K3f	f. Clouds
HI.III.C.K3g	g. Turbulence
HI.III.C.K3h	h. Thunderstorms and microbursts
HI.III.C.K3i	i. Icing and freezing level information
HI.III.C.K3j	j. Fog/mist
HI.III.C.K3k	k. Frost
HI.III.C.K3l	l. Obstructions to visibility (e.g., smoke, haze, volcanic ash, etc.)
HI.III.C.K4	Flight deck instrument displays of digital weather and aeronautical information.

Risk Management: The applicant explains and teaches how to identify and manage risk associated with:

HI.III.C.R1	Making the go/no-go and continue/divert decisions, including:
HI.III.C.R1a	a. Circumstances that would make diversion prudent
HI.III.C.R1b	b. Personal weather minimums
HI.III.C.R1c	c. Hazardous weather conditions, including known or forecast icing or turbulence aloft
HI.III.C.R2	Use and limitations of:
HI.III.C.R2a	a. Installed onboard weather equipment
HI.III.C.R2b	b. Aviation weather reports and forecasts
HI.III.C.R2c	c. Inflight weather resources

Skills: The applicant demonstrates and simultaneously explains how to:

HI.III.C.S1	Use available aviation weather resources to obtain an adequate weather briefing.
HI.III.C.S2	Analyze the implications of at least three of the conditions listed in K3a through K3l, using actual weather or weather conditions provided by the evaluator.
HI.III.C.S3	Correlate weather information to make a go/no-go decision.

Area of Operation IV. Preflight Lesson on a Maneuver to be Performed in Flight

Note: *The evaluator asks the applicant to present a preflight lesson on the selected maneuver as the lesson would be taught to a student and determines the outcome of this Task before the flight portion of the practical test. Previously developed lesson plans from the instructor applicant's library may be used.*

Task A. Maneuver Lesson

References: *FAA-H-8083-2, FAA-H-8083-4, FAA-H-8083-9, FAA-H-8083-21, FAA-H-8083-25; POH/RFM*

Objective: To determine the applicant understands the elements associated with a maneuver Task selected from Area of Operation VII (Hovering Maneuvers) through Area of Operation XII (Special Operations) and applies that knowledge when delivering ground instruction.

Knowledge:	The applicant demonstrates instructional knowledge by describing and explaining:
HI.IV.A.K1	Purpose of the maneuver.
HI.IV.A.K2	Elements of the maneuver and the associated common errors.
HI.IV.A.K3	Desired outcome(s), including completion standards.

Risk Management:	The applicant explains and teaches how to identify and manage risk associated with:
HI.IV.A.R1	The selected maneuver Task.

Skills:	The applicant exhibits the skill to:
HI.IV.A.S1	Deliver instruction on the selected maneuver using a lesson plan, teaching methods, and teaching aids, as appropriate, that incorporate K1 through K3.

Area of Operation V. Preflight Procedures

Note: *The evaluator must select at least one Task from this Area of Operation.*

Task A. Preflight Assessment

References: *AC 91-32; FAA-H-8083-2, FAA-H-8083-4, FAA-H-8083-9, FAA-H-8083-21, FAA-H-8083-25; POH/RFM*

Objective: To determine the applicant understands preflight assessment, can apply that knowledge, manage associated risks, demonstrate appropriate skills, and provide effective instruction.

Knowledge:	The applicant demonstrates instructional knowledge by describing and explaining:
HI.V.A.K1	Pilot self-assessment.
HI.V.A.K2	Determining that the helicopter to be used is appropriate and airworthy.
HI.V.A.K3	Helicopter preflight inspection, including:
HI.V.A.K3a	a. Which items should be inspected
HI.V.A.K3b	b. The reasons for checking each item
HI.V.A.K3c	c. How to detect possible defects
HI.V.A.K3d	d. The associated regulations
HI.V.A.K4	Environmental factors, including weather, terrain, route selection, and obstructions.

Risk Management:	The applicant explains and teaches how to identify and manage risk associated with:
HI.V.A.R1	Pilot.
HI.V.A.R2	Aircraft.
HI.V.A.R3	Environment (e.g., weather, icing, airports/heliports/helipads/landing areas, airspace, terrain, obstacles).
HI.V.A.R4	External pressures.
HI.V.A.R5	Aviation security concerns.

Skills:	The applicant demonstrates and simultaneously explains how to:
HI.V.A.S1	Inspect the helicopter with reference to an appropriate checklist.
HI.V.A.S2	Verify the helicopter is in condition for safe flight and conforms to its type design.
HI.V.A.S3	Perform self-assessment.
HI.V.A.S4	Continue to assess the environment for safe flight.

Task B. Flight Deck Management

References: *14 CFR part 91; AC 120-71; FAA-H-8083-2, FAA-H-8083-4, FAA-H-8083-9, FAA-H-8083-21, FAA-H-8083-25; POH/RFM*

Objective: To determine the applicant understands flight deck management, can apply that knowledge, manage associated risks, demonstrate appropriate skills, and provide effective instruction.

Note: *See Appendix 2: Safety of Flight.*

Knowledge:	The applicant demonstrates instructional knowledge by describing and explaining:
HI.V.B.K1	Passenger briefing requirements, including operation and required use of safety restraint systems.
HI.V.B.K2	Use of appropriate checklists.
HI.V.B.K3	Requirements for current and appropriate navigation data.
HI.V.B.K4	Securing items and cargo.

Risk Management:	The applicant explains and teaches how to identify and manage risk associated with:
HI.V.B.R1	Use of systems or equipment, including automation and portable electronic devices.
HI.V.B.R2	Inoperative equipment.
HI.V.B.R3	Passenger distractions.

Skills:	The applicant demonstrates and simultaneously explains how to:
HI.V.B.S1	Secure all items in the aircraft.
HI.V.B.S2	Conduct an appropriate passenger briefing, including identifying the pilot-in-command (PIC), use of safety belts, shoulder harnesses, doors, passenger conduct, rotor blade avoidance, and emergency procedures.
HI.V.B.S3	Properly program and manage helicopter automation, as applicable.
HI.V.B.S4	Appropriately manage risks by utilizing ADM, including SRM/CRM.

Task C. Powerplant Starting and Rotor Engagement

References:	FAA-H-8083-2, FAA-H-8083-4, FAA-H-8083-9, FAA-H-8083-21, FAA-H-8083-25; POH/RFM
Objective:	To determine the applicant understands powerplant starting and rotor engagement procedures can apply that knowledge, manage associated risks, demonstrate appropriate skills, and provide effective instruction.

Knowledge:	The applicant demonstrates instructional knowledge by describing and explaining:
HI.V.C.K1	Starting under various conditions.
HI.V.C.K2	Starting procedures, including the use of external power if applicable.
HI.V.C.K3	Limitations associated with starting.
HI.V.C.K4	Conditions leading to and procedures for an aborted start.

Risk Management:	The applicant explains and teaches how to identify and manage risk associated with:
HI.V.C.R1	Rotor engagement, if applicable.
HI.V.C.R2	Use of external power unit.
HI.V.C.R3	Limitations during starting.

Skills:	The applicant demonstrates and simultaneously explains how to:
HI.V.C.S1	Position the helicopter properly considering structures, surface conditions, other aircraft, wind, and the safety of nearby persons and property.

HI.V.C.S2	Use flight control frictions, if required.
HI.V.C.S3	Complete the appropriate checklist(s).
HI.V.C.S4	Engage and manage the rotor system, as appropriate.

Task D. Before Takeoff Check

References: FAA-H-8083-2, FAA-H-8083-4, FAA-H-8083-9, FAA-H-8083-21, FAA-H-8083-25; POH/RFM

Objective: To determine the applicant understands before takeoff checks, can apply that knowledge, manage associated risks, demonstrate appropriate skills, and provide effective instruction.

Knowledge:	The applicant demonstrates instructional knowledge by describing and explaining:
HI.V.D.K1	Purpose of before takeoff checklist items, including:
HI.V.D.K1a	a. Reasons for checking each item
HI.V.D.K1b	b. Detecting malfunctions
HI.V.D.K1c	c. Configuring the helicopter as recommended by the manufacturer

Risk Management:	The applicant explains and teaches how to identify and manage risk associated with:
HI.V.D.R1	Division of attention while conducting before takeoff checks.
HI.V.D.R2	Unexpected or unclear clearances from ATC.
HI.V.D.R3	Hazardous effects of downwash.

Skills:	The applicant demonstrates and simultaneously explains how to:
HI.V.D.S1	Complete the appropriate checklist(s).
HI.V.D.S2	Review takeoff performance and emergency procedures.
HI.V.D.S3	Verify that the powerplant temperature(s) and pressure(s) are suitable for takeoff.
HI.V.D.S4	Maintain powerplant and main rotor (Nr) speed within normal limits.
HI.V.D.S5	Divide attention inside and outside the helicopter.

Area of Operation VI. Airport and Heliport Operations

Note: *The evaluator must select at least one Task from this Area of Operation.*

Task A. Runway/Taxiway/Heliport/Helipad Signs, Markings, and Lighting

References: *14 CFR part 91; AIM; FAA-H-8083-2, FAA-H-8083-4, FAA-H-8083-9, FAA-H-8083-21, FAA-H-8083-25*

Objective: To determine the applicant understands airport/runway/ taxiway/heliport/helipad signs, markings, and lighting, can apply that knowledge, manage associated risks, demonstrate appropriate skills, and provide effective instruction.

Knowledge:	The applicant demonstrates instructional knowledge by describing and explaining:
HI.VI.A.K1	Airport runway, heliport, helipad, taxiway signs, markings, and lighting.
HI.VI.A.K2	Airport movement area.
HI.VI.A.K3	Common errors related to this Task.

Risk Management:	The applicant explains and teaches how to identify and manage risk associated with:
HI.VI.A.R1	Interpretation of signs, markings, or lighting.
HI.VI.A.R2	Landing site dimensions and limitations.
HI.VI.A.R3	Conflict with aircraft, vehicles, and persons.
HI.VI.A.R4	Distractions, task prioritization, loss of situational awareness, or disorientation.
HI.VI.A.R5	Runway incursion.

Skills:	The applicant demonstrates and simultaneously explains how to:
HI.VI.A.S1	Comply with airport/heliport/helipad signs, markings, and lighting encountered, as applicable to the helicopter provided for the practical test.
HI.VI.A.S2	Analyze and correct common errors related to this Task.

Task B. Communications, Light Signals, and Runway Lighting Systems

References: *14 CFR part 91; AIM; FAA-H-8083-2, FAA-H-8083-4, FAA-H-8083-9, FAA-H-8083-21, FAA-H-8083-25*

Objective: To determine the applicant understands communications and ATC light signals, can apply that knowledge, manage associated risks, demonstrate appropriate skills, and provide effective instruction.

Knowledge:	The applicant demonstrates instructional knowledge by describing and explaining:
HI.VI.B.K1	How to obtain appropriate radio frequencies.
HI.VI.B.K2	Proper radio communication procedures and air traffic control (ATC) phraseology.
HI.VI.B.K3	ATC light signal recognition.
HI.VI.B.K4	Appropriate use of transponder(s).
HI.VI.B.K5	Lost communication procedures.
HI.VI.B.K6	Equipment issues that could cause loss of communication.

HI.VI.B.K7	Radar assistance.
HI.VI.B.K8	Runway Status Lighting Systems.
HI.VI.B.K9	Common errors related to this Task.

Risk Management: The applicant explains and teaches how to identify and manage risk associated with:

HI.VI.B.R1	Communication.
HI.VI.B.R2	Deciding if and when to declare an emergency.
HI.VI.B.R3	Use of non-standard phraseology.

Skills: The applicant demonstrates and simultaneously explains how to:

HI.VI.B.S1	Select and activate appropriate frequencies.
HI.VI.B.S2	Transmit using standard phraseology and procedures as specified in the Aeronautical Information Manual (AIM) and Pilot/Controller Glossary.
HI.VI.B.S3	Acknowledge radio communications and comply with ATC instructions or as directed by the evaluator.
HI.VI.B.S4	Analyze and correct common errors related to this Task.

Task C. Traffic Patterns

References: 14 CFR part 91; AIM; FAA-H-8083-2, FAA-H-8083-4, FAA-H-8083-9, FAA-H-8083-21, FAA-H-8083-25

Objective: To determine the applicant understands traffic patterns, can apply that knowledge, manage associated risks, demonstrate appropriate skills, and provide effective instruction.

Knowledge: The applicant demonstrates instructional knowledge by describing and explaining:

HI.VI.C.K1	Towered and nontowered airport/heliport/helipad/landing area operations and restrictions.
HI.VI.C.K2	Traffic pattern for the current conditions.
HI.VI.C.K3	Right-of-way rules.
HI.VI.C.K4	Use of automated weather and airport/heliport information.
HI.VI.C.K5	Common errors related to this Task.

Risk Management: The applicant explains and teaches how to identify and manage risk associated with:

HI.VI.C.R1	Collision hazards.
HI.VI.C.R2	Distractions, task prioritization, loss of situational awareness, or disorientation.
HI.VI.C.R3	Windshear and wake turbulence.

Skills: The applicant demonstrates and simultaneously explains how to:

HI.VI.C.S1	Identify and interpret airport/heliport/helipad/landing area runways, taxiways, markings, signs, and lighting.
HI.VI.C.S2	Comply with recommended helicopter traffic pattern procedures, as appropriate.
HI.VI.C.S3	Correct for wind drift to maintain the proper ground track.

HI.VI.C.S4   Maintain orientation with the runway/landing area in use, as applicable.

HI.VI.C.S5   Maintain traffic pattern altitude, ±100 feet, and the appropriate airspeed, ±10 knots.

HI.VI.C.S6   Maintain situational awareness and proper spacing from other traffic or avoid the flow of fixed-wing traffic, as appropriate.

HI.VI.C.S7   Analyze and correct common errors related to this Task.

Area of Operation VII. Hovering Maneuvers

Note: *The evaluator must select at least one Task from this Area of Operation.*

Note: *Task D must be tested in addition to the other Tasks if the applicant supplies a helicopter with wheel-type landing gear.*

Task A. Vertical Takeoff and Landing

References: *14 CFR part 91; AC 90-95; FAA-H-8083-2, FAA-H-8083-4, FAA-H-8083-9, FAA-H-8083-21, FAA-H-8083-25; POH/RFM*

Objective: To determine the applicant understands vertical takeoff and landing from a hover, can apply that knowledge, manage associated risks, demonstrate appropriate skills, and provide effective instruction.

Knowledge:	The applicant demonstrates instructional knowledge by describing and explaining:
HI.VII.A.K1	Elements related to a vertical takeoff to a hover and landing from a hover.
HI.VII.A.K2	Effect of wind on flight control inputs.
HI.VII.A.K3	Effect of weight and balance and various centers of gravity.
HI.VII.A.K4	Ground effect.
HI.VII.A.K5	Common errors related to this Task.

Risk Management:	The applicant explains and teaches how to identify and manage risk associated with:
HI.VII.A.R1	Loss of tail rotor effectiveness (LTE).
HI.VII.A.R2	Dynamic rollover.
HI.VII.A.R3	Ground resonance.
HI.VII.A.R4	Powerplant failure during hover.

Skills:	The applicant demonstrates and simultaneously explains how to:
HI.VII.A.S1	Complete the appropriate checklist(s).
HI.VII.A.S2	Comply with air traffic control (ATC) or evaluator instructions and make radio calls as appropriate.
HI.VII.A.S3	Maintain powerplant and main rotor (Nr) speed within normal limits.
HI.VII.A.S4	Ascend to and maintain recommended hovering altitude, and descend from recommended hovering altitude in headwind, crosswind, and tailwind conditions, without drift.
HI.VII.A.S5	Maintain recommended hovering altitude, ±1/2 of that altitude within 10 feet of the surface, if above 10 feet, ±5 feet.
HI.VII.A.S6	Maintain position within 2 feet of a designated point with no aft movement.
HI.VII.A.S7	Descend vertically to within 2 feet of the designated touchdown point.
HI.VII.A.S8	Maintain specified heading, ± 10°.
HI.VII.A.S9	Analyze and correct common errors related to this Task.

Task B. Hover Taxi

References: *AC 91-73; AIM; Chart Supplements; FAA-H-8083-2, FAA-H-8083-4, FAA-H-8083-9, FAA-H-8083-21, FAA-H-8083-25; POH/RFM*

Objective: To determine the applicant understands hover taxi operations, can apply that knowledge, manage associated risks, demonstrate appropriate skills, and provide effective instruction.

Knowledge:	The applicant demonstrates instructional knowledge by describing and explaining:
HI.VII.B.K1	Current airport aeronautical references and information resources such as the Chart Supplement, airport diagram, and Notices to Air Missions (NOTAMs).
HI.VII.B.K2	Hover taxi instructions, clearances, and limitations.
HI.VII.B.K3	Airport/heliport/helipad/landing area, signs, markings, and lighting.
HI.VII.B.K4	Visual indicators for wind.
HI.VII.B.K5	Aircraft lighting, as appropriate.
HI.VII.B.K6	Procedures for:
HI.VII.B.K6a	a. Pilot activities during taxiing
HI.VII.B.K6b	b. Safe hover taxi at towered and non-towered airports/heliports/helipads/landing areas
HI.VII.B.K6c	c. Entering or crossing runways
HI.VII.B.K7	Height/Velocity (H/V) considerations.
HI.VII.B.K8	Aircraft operating limitations.
HI.VII.B.K9	Common errors related to this Task.

Risk Management:	The applicant explains and teaches how to identify and manage risk associated with:
HI.VII.B.R1	Distractions, task prioritization, loss of situational awareness, or disorientation.
HI.VII.B.R2	Reduced visibility or night taxi operations.
HI.VII.B.R3	Runway incursion.
HI.VII.B.R4	Other aircraft, vehicles, persons, and hazards.
HI.VII.B.R5	Hazardous effects of downwash.
HI.VII.B.R6	Main rotor, tail rotor, and tail strike hazards.
HI.VII.B.R7	Height/Velocity (H/V) considerations.
HI.VII.B.R8	Confirmation or expectation bias as related to taxi instructions.

Skills:	The applicant demonstrates and simultaneously explains how to:
HI.VII.B.S1	Complete the appropriate checklist(s).
HI.VII.B.S2	Receive and correctly read back clearances/instructions, if applicable.
HI.VII.B.S3	Use an airport diagram or taxi chart during taxi, if published, and maintain situational awareness.
HI.VII.B.S4	Comply with airport/heliport taxiway markings, signals, and signs.
HI.VII.B.S5	Maintain powerplant and main rotor (Nr) speed within normal limits.
HI.VII.B.S6	Maintain a straight ground track within ±2 feet of a designated ground track.

HI.VII.B.S7	Maintain recommended hovering altitude, ±1/2 of that altitude within 10 feet of the surface, if above 10 feet, ±5 feet.
HI.VII.B.S8	Hover taxi over specified ground references, demonstrating forward, sideward, and rearward hovering and hovering turns.
HI.VII.B.S9	Maintain a constant rate of turn at pivot points.
HI.VII.B.S10	Maintain a position within 2 feet of each pivot point during turns.
HI.VII.B.S11	Make a 360° pivoting turn, left and right, stopping within 10° of a specified heading.
HI.VII.B.S12	Make smooth, timely, and correct control application during the maneuver.
HI.VII.B.S13	Analyze and correct common errors related to this Task.

Task C. Air Taxi

References: AC 91-73; AIM; Chart Supplements; FAA-H-8083-2, FAA-H-8083-4, FAA-H-8083-9, FAA-H-8083-21, FAA-H-8083-25; POH/RFM

Objective: To determine the applicant understands air taxi operations, can apply that knowledge, manage associated risks, demonstrate appropriate skills, and provide effective instruction.

Knowledge:	The applicant demonstrates instructional knowledge by describing and explaining:
HI.VII.C.K1	Current airport aeronautical references and information resources such as the Chart Supplement, airport diagram, and Notices to Air Missions (NOTAMs).
HI.VII.C.K2	Air taxi instructions, clearances, and limitations.
HI.VII.C.K3	Airport/heliport/helipad/landing area, signs, markings, and lighting.
HI.VII.C.K4	Visual indicators for wind.
HI.VII.C.K5	Aircraft lighting, as appropriate.
HI.VII.C.K6	Procedures for:
HI.VII.C.K6a	a. Pilot activities during taxiing
HI.VII.C.K6b	b. Safe air taxi at towered and nontowered airports
HI.VII.C.K6c	c. Overflying of runways
HI.VII.C.K7	Height/Velocity (H/V) considerations.
HI.VII.C.K8	Common errors related to this Task.

Risk Management:	The applicant explains and teaches how to identify and manage risk associated with:
HI.VII.C.R1	Distractions, task prioritization, loss of situational awareness, or disorientation.
HI.VII.C.R2	Reduced visibility or night taxi operations.
HI.VII.C.R3	Runway incursion.
HI.VII.C.R4	Main rotor, tail rotor, and tail strike hazards.
HI.VII.C.R5	H/V diagram performance in case of powerplant failure.
HI.VII.C.R6	Confirmation or expectation bias as related to taxi instructions.

Skills:	The applicant demonstrates and simultaneously explains how to:
HI.VII.C.S1	Complete the appropriate checklist(s).

HI.VII.C.S2	Use an airport diagram or taxi chart during taxi, if published, and maintain situational awareness.
HI.VII.C.S3	Select a safe airspeed and altitude.
HI.VII.C.S4	Maintain desired track and groundspeed in headwind and crosswind conditions, avoiding conditions that might lead to loss of tail rotor/antitorque effectiveness.
HI.VII.C.S5	Maintain powerplant and main rotor (Nr) speed within normal limits.
HI.VII.C.S6	Comply with airport/heliport/helipad/landing area markings, lights, signs, and ATC instructions.
HI.VII.C.S7	Maintain specified altitude, ±10 feet.
HI.VII.C.S8	Analyze and correct common errors related to this Task.

Task D. Taxiing with Wheel-Type Landing Gear

References: AC 91-73; AIM; Chart Supplements; FAA-H-8083-2, FAA-H-8083-4, FAA-H-8083-9, FAA-H-8083-21, FAA-H-8083-25; POH/RFM

Objective: To determine the applicant understands taxiing with wheel-type landing gear, can apply that knowledge, manage associated risks, demonstrate appropriate skills, and provide effective instruction.

Knowledge: The applicant demonstrates instructional knowledge by describing and explaining:

HI.VII.D.K1	Current airport aeronautical references and information resources such as the Chart Supplement, airport diagram, and Notices to Air Missions (NOTAMs).
HI.VII.D.K2	Taxi instructions/clearances.
HI.VII.D.K3	Airport/heliport/helipad/landing area, signs, markings, and lighting.
HI.VII.D.K4	Visual indicators for wind.
HI.VII.D.K5	Aircraft lighting, as appropriate.
HI.VII.D.K6	Procedures for:
HI.VII.D.K6a	a. Appropriate flight deck activities prior to taxi, including route planning and identifying the location of Hot Spots
HI.VII.D.K6b	b. Safe taxi at towered and nontowered airports
HI.VII.D.K6c	c. Entering or crossing runways
HI.VII.D.K7	Common errors related to this Task.

Risk Management: The applicant explains and teaches how to identify and manage risk associated with:

HI.VII.D.R1	Activities and distractions.
HI.VII.D.R2	Confirmation or expectation bias as related to taxi instructions.
HI.VII.D.R3	Runway incursion.
HI.VII.D.R4	Speed during taxi and turns.
HI.VII.D.R5	Appropriate thrust vector and brake use.
HI.VII.D.R6	Airframe and rotor clearances during taxi.

Skills: The applicant demonstrates and simultaneously explains how to:

HI.VII.D.S1	Complete the appropriate checklist(s).

HI.VII.D.S2	Use an appropriate airport/heliport diagram or taxi chart, if published.
HI.VII.D.S3	Properly position nosewheel/tailwheel, if applicable, locked or unlocked.
HI.VII.D.S4	Position the flight controls properly for the existing wind conditions, with the landing gear in contact with the surface, avoiding conditions that might lead to loss of directional control.
HI.VII.D.S5	Properly use cyclic, collective, and brakes as applicable to control speed while taxiing.
HI.VII.D.S6	Maintain powerplant and main rotor (Nr) speed within normal limits.
HI.VII.D.S7	Maintain specified track within 2 feet.
HI.VII.D.S8	Position the helicopter relative to hold lines or a specified point.
HI.VII.D.S9	Receive and comply with ATC clearances/instructions, if applicable.
HI.VII.D.S10	Comply with airport/heliport taxiway markings, lights, and signals.
HI.VII.D.S11	Analyze and correct common errors related to this Task.

Task E. Slope Operations

References: FAA-H-8083-2, FAA-H-8083-4, FAA-H-8083-9, FAA-H-8083-21, FAA-H-8083-25; POH/RFM

Objective: To determine the applicant understands slope operations, can apply that knowledge, manage associated risks, demonstrate appropriate skills, and provide effective instruction.

Note: See Appendix 3: Aircraft, Equipment, and Operational Requirements & Limitations for information related to this Task.

Knowledge:	The applicant demonstrates instructional knowledge by describing and explaining:
HI.VII.E.K1	Elements related to slope operations.
HI.VII.E.K2	Factors used for selecting an appropriate slope.
HI.VII.E.K3	Effect of wind on slope operations.
HI.VII.E.K4	Dynamic rollover considerations during slope operations and preventive/recovery techniques.
HI.VII.E.K5	Helicopter slope limitations.
HI.VII.E.K6	Common errors related to this Task.

Risk Management:	The applicant explains and teaches how to identify and manage risk associated with:
HI.VII.E.R1	Operations on a slope.
HI.VII.E.R2	Conditions leading to loss of tail rotor/antitorque effectiveness.
HI.VII.E.R3	Embarking or disembarking passengers and rotor blade hazards.
HI.VII.E.R4	Conditions leading to dynamic rollover.
HI.VII.E.R5	Surface conditions.
HI.VII.E.R6	Collision hazards.
HI.VII.E.R7	Exceeding the manufacturer's slope limitations.

Skills:	The applicant demonstrates and simultaneously explains how to:
HI.VII.E.S1	Select a suitable slope.
HI.VII.E.S2	Complete the appropriate checklist(s).

HI.VII.E.S3	Properly approach the slope considering wind effect and obstacles.
HI.VII.E.S4	Maintain powerplant and main rotor (Nr) speed within normal limits.
HI.VII.E.S5	Maintain heading and ground position and prevent movement of aircraft on slope.
HI.VII.E.S6	Make a smooth positive descent to touch the upslope skid or wheel(s) on the sloping surface.
HI.VII.E.S7	Recognize if slope is too steep and abandon the operation prior to reaching cyclic control stops.
HI.VII.E.S8	Maintain positive control while lowering the downslope skid or wheel to touchdown.
HI.VII.E.S9	Neutralize controls after landing.
HI.VII.E.S10	Make a smooth transition from the slope to a stabilized hover parallel to the slope.
HI.VII.E.S11	Properly move away from the slope.
HI.VII.E.S12	Maintain a specified heading throughout the operation, ±5°.
HI.VII.E.S13	Analyze and correct common errors related to this Task.

Area of Operation VIII. Takeoffs, Landings, and Go-Arounds

Note: *The evaluator must select at least one takeoff and one approach Task from Area of Operation VIII, Takeoffs, Landings, and Go-Arounds.*

Note: *Task E must be tested in addition to the other Tasks if the applicant supplies a helicopter with wheel-type landing gear.*

Task A. Normal Takeoff and Climb

References: FAA-H-8083-2, FAA-H-8083-4, FAA-H-8083-9, FAA-H-8083-21, FAA-H-8083-25; POH/RFM

Objective: To determine the applicant understands normal takeoff, climb operations, and rejected takeoff procedures, can apply that knowledge, manage associated risks, demonstrate appropriate skills, and provide effective instruction.

Note: *If a crosswind condition does not exist, the applicant's knowledge of crosswind elements must be evaluated through oral testing.*

Knowledge:	The applicant demonstrates instructional knowledge by describing and explaining:
HI.VIII.A.K1	Effects of atmospheric conditions, including wind, on takeoff and climb performance.
HI.VIII.A.K2	Factors affecting the profile of the height/velocity (H/V) diagram.
HI.VIII.A.K3	Common errors related to this Task.

Risk Management:	The applicant explains and teaches how to identify and manage risk associated with:
HI.VIII.A.R1	Selection of takeoff path based on helicopter performance and limitations, available distance, and wind.
HI.VIII.A.R2	Effects of:
HI.VIII.A.R2a	a. Crosswind
HI.VIII.A.R2b	b. Windshear
HI.VIII.A.R2c	c. Tailwind
HI.VIII.A.R2d	d. Turbulence, including wake turbulence
HI.VIII.A.R2e	e. Runway/departure point surface/condition
HI.VIII.A.R3	Abnormal operations, including planning for:
HI.VIII.A.R3a	a. Rejected takeoff
HI.VIII.A.R3b	b. Powerplant failure in takeoff/climb phase of flight
HI.VIII.A.R4	Collision hazards.
HI.VIII.A.R5	Distractions, task prioritization, loss of situational awareness, or disorientation.
HI.VIII.A.R6	Runway incursion.

Skills:	The applicant demonstrates and simultaneously explains how to:
HI.VIII.A.S1	Complete the appropriate checklist(s).
HI.VIII.A.S2	Make radio calls as appropriate.
HI.VIII.A.S3	Verify assigned/correct runway, if at an airport.
HI.VIII.A.S4	Determine wind direction with or without visible wind direction indicators.

HI.VIII.A.S5	Clear the area, taxi into the takeoff position, and align the helicopter on the runway centerline or with takeoff path.
HI.VIII.A.S6	Establish a stationary position on the surface or a stabilized hover prior to takeoff in headwind and crosswind conditions.
HI.VIII.A.S7	Confirm takeoff power and instrument indications prior to forward movement.
HI.VIII.A.S8	After clearing all obstacles, transition to normal climb attitude, airspeed, ±5 knots, and power setting.
HI.VIII.A.S9	Maintain powerplant and main rotor (Nr) speed within normal limits.
HI.VIII.A.S10	Maintain proper ground track with crosswind correction, as needed.
HI.VIII.A.S11	Comply with noise abatement procedures, as applicable.
HI.VIII.A.S12	Use runway incursion avoidance procedures, if applicable.
HI.VIII.A.S13	Analyze and correct common errors related to this Task.

Task B. Normal and Crosswind Approach

References: AIM; FAA-H-8083-2, FAA-H-8083-4, FAA-H-8083-9, FAA-H-8083-21, FAA-H-8083-25; POH/RFM

Objective: To determine the applicant understands normal and crosswind approach, can apply that knowledge, manage associated risks, demonstrate appropriate skills, and provide effective instruction.

Note: If a crosswind condition does not exist, the applicant's knowledge of crosswind elements must be evaluated through oral testing.

Knowledge:	The applicant demonstrates instructional knowledge by describing and explaining:
HI.VIII.B.K1	Effects of wind, weight, altitude, and temperature on performance.
HI.VIII.B.K2	Wind correction techniques on approach and landing.
HI.VIII.B.K3	Landing surface, obstructions, and selection of a suitable touchdown point.
HI.VIII.B.K4	Factors affecting the profile of the height/velocity (H/V) diagram.
HI.VIII.B.K5	Common errors related to this Task.

Risk Management:	The applicant explains and teaches how to identify and manage risk associated with:
HI.VIII.B.R1	Selection of approach path and landing based on aircraft performance and limitations, and wind.
HI.VIII.B.R2	Effects of:
HI.VIII.B.R2a	a. Crosswind
HI.VIII.B.R2b	b. Windshear
HI.VIII.B.R2c	c. Tailwind
HI.VIII.B.R2d	d. Turbulence, including wake turbulence
HI.VIII.B.R2e	e. Vortex ring state (VRS)
HI.VIII.B.R2f	f. Touchdown surface and condition
HI.VIII.B.R3	Go-around/rejected landing.

HI.VIII.B.R4	Collision hazards.
HI.VIII.B.R5	Distractions, task prioritization, loss of situational awareness, or disorientation.
HI.VIII.B.R6	Loss of tail rotor effectiveness (LTE).

Skills:	The applicant demonstrates and simultaneously explains how to:
HI.VIII.B.S1	Complete the appropriate checklist(s).
HI.VIII.B.S2	Make radio calls as appropriate.
HI.VIII.B.S3	Determine wind direction with or without visible wind direction indicators.
HI.VIII.B.S4	Align the helicopter with the correct/assigned runway or touchdown point.
HI.VIII.B.S5	Scan the landing area/touchdown point and adjoining area for traffic and obstructions.
HI.VIII.B.S6	Maintain proper ground track with crosswind correction, if necessary.
HI.VIII.B.S7	Establish and maintain a normal approach angle and rate of closure.
HI.VIII.B.S8	Maintain powerplant and main rotor (Nr) speed within normal limits.
HI.VIII.B.S9	Arrive at the termination point, on the surface or at a stabilized hover ±2 feet.
HI.VIII.B.S10	Use runway incursion avoidance procedures, if applicable.
HI.VIII.B.S11	Analyze and correct common errors related to this Task.

Task C. Maximum Performance Takeoff and Climb

References: AIM; FAA-H-8083-2, FAA-H-8083-4, FAA-H-8083-9, FAA-H-8083-21, FAA-H-8083-25; POH/RFM

Objective: To determine the applicant understands maximum performance takeoff and climb, can apply that knowledge, manage associated risks, demonstrate appropriate skills, and provide effective instruction.

Knowledge:	The applicant demonstrates instructional knowledge by describing and explaining:
HI.VIII.C.K1	Situations where this maneuver is appropriate.
HI.VIII.C.K2	Effects of atmospheric conditions, including wind and temperature, on takeoff and climb performance.
HI.VIII.C.K3	Powerplant failure during approach/landing phase of flight.
HI.VIII.C.K4	Common errors related to this Task.

Risk Management:	The applicant explains and teaches how to identify and manage risk associated with:
HI.VIII.C.R1	Selection of takeoff path based on helicopter performance and limitations, available distance, and wind.
HI.VIII.C.R2	Effects of:
HI.VIII.C.R2a	a. Crosswind
HI.VIII.C.R2b	b. Windshear
HI.VIII.C.R2c	c. Tailwind
HI.VIII.C.R2d	d. Turbulence, including wake turbulence
HI.VIII.C.R2e	e. Surface conditions

HI.VIII.C.R3	Abnormal operations including:
HI.VIII.C.R3a	a. Rejected takeoff
HI.VIII.C.R3b	b. Powerplant failure in takeoff/climb phase of flight
HI.VIII.C.R4	Collision hazards.
HI.VIII.C.R5	Low rotor rpm.
HI.VIII.C.R6	Distractions, task prioritization, loss of situational awareness, or disorientation.

Skills:	The applicant demonstrates and simultaneously explains how to:
HI.VIII.C.S1	Complete the appropriate checklist(s).
HI.VIII.C.S2	Make radio calls as appropriate.
HI.VIII.C.S3	Use control inputs to initiate lift-off from the takeoff position using a forward climb attitude to fly the departure profile.
HI.VIII.C.S4	Maintain powerplant and rotor rpm within normal limits.
HI.VIII.C.S5	Use required takeoff power, or power as specified by the evaluator.
HI.VIII.C.S6	After clearing all obstacles, transition to normal climb attitude, airspeed, ±5 knots, and power setting.
HI.VIII.C.S7	Maintain directional control, ground track, and proper wind-drift correction throughout the maneuver.
HI.VIII.C.S8	Analyze and correct common errors related to this Task.

Task D. Steep Approach

References: AIM; FAA-H-8083-2, FAA-H-8083-4, FAA-H-8083-9, FAA-H-8083-21, FAA-H-8083-25; POH/RFM

Objective: To determine the applicant understands steep approaches, can apply that knowledge, manage associated risks, demonstrate appropriate skills, and provide effective instruction.

Knowledge:	The applicant demonstrates instructional knowledge by describing and explaining:
HI.VIII.D.K1	A stabilized steep approach.
HI.VIII.D.K2	Approach techniques and applicability.
HI.VIII.D.K3	Performance data and the height velocity (H/V) diagram.
HI.VIII.D.K4	Effects of atmospheric conditions on approach and landing performance.
HI.VIII.D.K5	Wind correction techniques.
HI.VIII.D.K6	Aircraft performance and limitations.
HI.VIII.D.K7	Common errors related to this Task.

Risk Management:	The applicant explains and teaches how to identify and manage risk associated with:
HI.VIII.D.R1	Selection of approach path and landing based on aircraft performance and limitations, and wind.
HI.VIII.D.R2	Effects of:
HI.VIII.D.R2a	a. Wind Direction

HI.VIII.D.R2b	b. Windshear
HI.VIII.D.R2c	c. Turbulence, including wake turbulence
HI.VIII.D.R3	Planning for:
HI.VIII.D.R3a	a. Rejected landing and go-around
HI.VIII.D.R3b	b. Powerplant failure during the approach
HI.VIII.D.R4	Collision hazards.
HI.VIII.D.R5	Vortex ring state (VRS).
HI.VIII.D.R6	Landing surface.
HI.VIII.D.R7	Aircraft limitations.
HI.VIII.D.R8	Distractions, task prioritization, loss of situational awareness, or disorientation.
HI.VIII.D.R9	Loss of tail rotor effectiveness (LTE).
HI.VIII.D.R10	Degraded Visual Environment (DVE) and flat light conditions.

Skills:	The applicant demonstrates and simultaneously explains how to:
HI.VIII.D.S1	Complete the appropriate checklist(s).
HI.VIII.D.S2	Make radio calls as appropriate.
HI.VIII.D.S3	Consider the wind direction and conditions, landing surface, and obstacles.
HI.VIII.D.S4	Select a suitable termination point.
HI.VIII.D.S5	Establish and maintain a steep approach angle, (15° maximum) and proper rate of closure.
HI.VIII.D.S6	Maintain proper ground track with crosswind correction, if necessary.
HI.VIII.D.S7	Maintain powerplant and main rotor (Nr) speed within normal limits.
HI.VIII.D.S8	Arrive at the termination point, on the surface or at a stabilized hover ±2 feet.
HI.VIII.D.S9	Use runway incursion avoidance procedures, if applicable.
HI.VIII.D.S10	Analyze and correct common errors related to this Task.

Task E. Rolling Takeoff (Wheel-Type Landing Gear)

References: FAA-H-8083-2, FAA-H-8083-4, FAA-H-8083-9, FAA-H-8083-21, FAA-H-8083-25; POH/RFM

Objective: To determine the applicant understands rolling takeoff with wheel-type landing gear, can apply that knowledge, manage associated risks, demonstrate appropriate skills, and provide effective instruction.

Note: If a crosswind condition does not exist, the applicant's knowledge of crosswind elements must be evaluated through oral testing.

Knowledge:	The applicant demonstrates instructional knowledge by describing and explaining:
HI.VIII.E.K1	Elements of a rolling takeoff.
HI.VIII.E.K2	Effects of wind, weight, temperature, and density altitude.
HI.VIII.E.K3	Situations when a rolling takeoff is recommended and factors related to takeoff and climb performance.
HI.VIII.E.K4	Translational lift.

| HI.VIII.E.K5 | Common errors related to this Task. |

Risk Management: The applicant explains and teaches how to identify and manage risk associated with:

HI.VIII.E.R1	Selection of takeoff path based on helicopter performance and limitations, available distance, and wind.
HI.VIII.E.R2	Effects of:
HI.VIII.E.R2a	a. Wind Direction
HI.VIII.E.R2b	b. Windshear
HI.VIII.E.R2c	c. Turbulence, including wake turbulence
HI.VIII.E.R3	Planning for:
HI.VIII.E.R3a	a. Height/Velocity (H/V) considerations
HI.VIII.E.R3b	b. Rejected takeoff
HI.VIII.E.R3c	c. Powerplant failure during takeoff/climb phase of flight
HI.VIII.E.R4	Collision hazards.
HI.VIII.E.R5	Takeoff surface.
HI.VIII.E.R6	Landing gear.
HI.VIII.E.R7	Distractions, task prioritization, loss of situational awareness, or disorientation.

Skills: The applicant demonstrates and simultaneously explains how to:

HI.VIII.E.S1	Complete the appropriate checklist(s).
HI.VIII.E.S2	Make radio calls as appropriate.
HI.VIII.E.S3	Determine wind direction with or without visible wind direction indicators.
HI.VIII.E.S4	Verify assigned/correct takeoff path.
HI.VIII.E.S5	Maintain powerplant and main rotor (Nr) speed within normal limits.
HI.VIII.E.S6	Use control inputs that initiate the takeoff roll.
HI.VIII.E.S7	Maintain proper ground track with crosswind correction, while accelerating.
HI.VIII.E.S8	Transition to a normal climb airspeed, ±5 knots, and set appropriate power.
HI.VIII.E.S9	Maintain proper ground track with crosswind correction after liftoff.
HI.VIII.E.S10	Use runway incursion avoidance procedures, if applicable.
HI.VIII.E.S11	Analyze and correct common errors related to this Task.

Task F. Shallow Approach and Running/Roll-On Landing

References: FAA-H-8083-2, FAA-H-8083-4, FAA-H-8083-9, FAA-H-8083-21, FAA-H-8083-25; POH/RFM

Objective: To determine the applicant understands shallow approach and running/roll-on landing, can apply that knowledge, manage associated risks, demonstrate appropriate skills, and provide effective instruction.

Knowledge:	The applicant demonstrates instructional knowledge by describing and explaining:
HI.VIII.F.K1	Elements related to shallow approach and running/roll-on landing, including when to use the maneuver, aircraft limitations, and effect of landing surface texture.
HI.VIII.F.K2	Effects of wind, weight, temperature, and density altitude.
HI.VIII.F.K3	Common errors related to this Task.

Risk Management:	The applicant explains and teaches how to identify and manage risk associated with:
HI.VIII.F.R1	Selection of approach path and landing based on aircraft performance and limitations, and wind.
HI.VIII.F.R2	Effects of:
HI.VIII.F.R2a	a. Wind Direction
HI.VIII.F.R2b	b. Windshear
HI.VIII.F.R2c	c. Turbulence, including wake turbulence
HI.VIII.F.R3	Planning for:
HI.VIII.F.R3a	a. Powerplant failure during approach/landing phase of flight
HI.VIII.F.R4	Collision hazards.
HI.VIII.F.R5	Landing surface.
HI.VIII.F.R6	Dynamic rollover.
HI.VIII.F.R7	Ground resonance.
HI.VIII.F.R8	Aircraft limitations.
HI.VIII.F.R9	Distractions, task prioritization, loss of situational awareness, or disorientation.

Skills:	The applicant demonstrates and simultaneously explains how to:
HI.VIII.F.S1	Complete the appropriate checklist(s).
HI.VIII.F.S2	Make radio calls as appropriate.
HI.VIII.F.S3	Maintain powerplant and main rotor (Nr) speed within normal limits.
HI.VIII.F.S4	Establish and maintain the recommended approach angle and proper rate of closure.
HI.VIII.F.S5	Determine wind direction and maintain ground track with crosswind correction.
HI.VIII.F.S6	Maintain effective translational lift during surface contact with landing gear parallel to the ground track.
HI.VIII.F.S7	Make smooth, timely, and correct control inputs after surface contact to maintain directional control.
HI.VIII.F.S8	Use runway incursion avoidance procedures, if applicable.
HI.VIII.F.S9	Analyze and correct common errors related to this Task.

Task G. Go-Around

References: FAA-H-8083-2, FAA-H-8083-4, FAA-H-8083-9, FAA-H-8083-21, FAA-H-8083-25; POH/RFM

Objective: To determine the applicant understands go-around with emphasis on factors that contribute to landing conditions that may require a go-around, can apply that knowledge, manage associated risks, demonstrate appropriate skills, and provide effective instruction.

Knowledge:	The applicant demonstrates instructional knowledge by describing and explaining:
HI.VIII.G.K1	Situations and considerations on approach that could require a go-around.
HI.VIII.G.K2	Effects of atmospheric conditions on a go-around.
HI.VIII.G.K3	Go-around procedures and the importance of a timely decision.
HI.VIII.G.K4	Common errors related to this Task.

Risk Management:	The applicant explains and teaches how to identify and manage risk associated with:
HI.VIII.G.R1	Recognition of the need for a go-around.
HI.VIII.G.R2	Application of power and flight control inputs.
HI.VIII.G.R3	Collision hazards.
HI.VIII.G.R4	Distractions, task prioritization, loss of situational awareness, or disorientation.
HI.VIII.G.R5	Runway incursion.

Skills:	The applicant demonstrates and simultaneously explains how to:
HI.VIII.G.S1	Make a timely decision to discontinue the approach or at the direction of the evaluator.
HI.VIII.G.S2	Maintain powerplant and rotor rpm within normal limits while applying proper control input to stop descent and initiate climb.
HI.VIII.G.S3	Transition to a positive rate of climb and appropriate airspeed of ±5 knots.
HI.VIII.G.S4	Maintain directional control, ground track, and proper wind-drift correction throughout the maneuver.
HI.VIII.G.S5	Notify/coordinate with air traffic control (ATC) or evaluator instructions as required.
HI.VIII.G.S6	Complete the appropriate checklist(s).
HI.VIII.G.S7	Use single-pilot resource management (SRM) or crew resource management (CRM), as appropriate.
HI.VIII.G.S8	Use runway incursion avoidance procedures, if applicable.
HI.VIII.G.S9	Analyze and correct common errors related to this Task.

Area of Operation IX. Fundamentals of Flight

Note: *The evaluator must select at least one Task from this Area of Operation.*

Task A. Straight-and-Level Flight

References: *FAA-H-8083-2, FAA-H-8083-4, FAA-H-8083-9, FAA-H-8083-21, FAA-H-8083-25*

Objective: To determine the applicant understands straight-and-level flight, can apply that knowledge, manage associated risks, demonstrate appropriate skills, and provide effective instruction.

Knowledge:	The applicant demonstrates instructional knowledge by describing and explaining:
HI.IX.A.K1	Basic elements of the aircraft and aerodynamics that affect the ability to maintain straight-and-level flight.
HI.IX.A.K2	Flight control and trim use, if applicable.
HI.IX.A.K3	The pilot's visual references when performing the maneuver.
HI.IX.A.K4	Integrated flight instruction.
HI.IX.A.K5	Common errors related to this Task.

Risk Management:	The applicant explains and teaches how to identify and manage risk associated with:
HI.IX.A.R1	Distractions, task prioritization, loss of situational awareness, or disorientation.
HI.IX.A.R2	Collision hazards.

Skills:	The applicant demonstrates and simultaneously explains how to:
HI.IX.A.S1	Establish and maintain straight-and-level flight.
HI.IX.A.S2	Analyze and correct common errors related to this Task.

Task B. Level Turns

References: *FAA-H-8083-2, FAA-H-8083-4, FAA-H-8083-9, FAA-H-8083-21, FAA-H-8083-25*

Objective: To determine the applicant understands level turns, can apply that knowledge, manage associated risks, demonstrate appropriate skills, and provide effective instruction.

Knowledge:	The applicant demonstrates instructional knowledge by describing and explaining:
HI.IX.B.K1	Purpose of and procedures for level turns.
HI.IX.B.K2	Flight control and trim use, if applicable.
HI.IX.B.K3	The pilot's visual references when performing the maneuver.
HI.IX.B.K4	Integrated flight instruction.
HI.IX.B.K5	Common errors related to this Task.

Risk Management:	The applicant explains and teaches how to identify and manage risk associated with:
HI.IX.B.R1	Distractions, task prioritization, loss of situational awareness, or disorientation.
HI.IX.B.R2	Collision hazards.

Skills:	The applicant demonstrates and simultaneously explains how to:
HI.IX.B.S1	Establish, maintain, and roll out of a level turn.
HI.IX.B.S2	Analyze and correct common errors related to this Task.

Task C. Straight Climbs and Climbing Turns

References: FAA-H-8083-2, FAA-H-8083-4, FAA-H-8083-9, FAA-H-8083-21, FAA-H-8083-25

Objective: To determine the applicant understands straight climbs and climbing turns, can apply that knowledge, manage associated risks, demonstrate appropriate skills, and provide effective instruction.

Knowledge:	The applicant demonstrates instructional knowledge by describing and explaining:
HI.IX.C.K1	Purpose of and procedures for straight climbs and climbing turns.
HI.IX.C.K2	Flight control and trim use, if applicable.
HI.IX.C.K3	The pilot's visual references when performing the maneuver.
HI.IX.C.K4	Integrated flight instruction.
HI.IX.C.K5	Common errors related to this Task.

Risk Management:	The applicant explains and teaches how to identify and manage risk associated with:
HI.IX.C.R1	Distractions, task prioritization, loss of situational awareness, or disorientation.
HI.IX.C.R2	Collision hazards.

Skills:	The applicant demonstrates and simultaneously explains how to:
HI.IX.C.S1	Establish, maintain, and level off from climbs and climbing turns.
HI.IX.C.S2	Analyze and correct common errors related to this Task.

Task D. Straight Descents and Descending Turns

References: FAA-H-8083-2, FAA-H-8083-4, FAA-H-8083-9, FAA-H-8083-21, FAA-H-8083-25

Objective: To determine the applicant understands straight descents and descending turns, can apply that knowledge, manage associated risks, demonstrate appropriate skills, and provide effective instruction.

Knowledge:	The applicant demonstrates instructional knowledge by describing and explaining:
HI.IX.D.K1	Purpose of and procedures for straight descents and descending turns.
HI.IX.D.K2	Flight control and trim use, if applicable.
HI.IX.D.K3	The pilot's visual references when performing the maneuver.
HI.IX.D.K4	Integrated flight instruction.
HI.IX.D.K5	Common errors related to this Task.

Risk
Management: The applicant explains and teaches how to identify and manage risk associated with:

HI.IX.D.R1   Distractions, task prioritization, loss of situational awareness, or disorientation.

HI.IX.D.R2   Collision hazards.

Skills: The applicant demonstrates and simultaneously explains how to:

HI.IX.D.S1   Establish, maintain, and level off from straight descents and descending turns.

HI.IX.D.S2   Analyze and correct common errors related to this Task.

Area of Operation X. Performance Maneuvers

Note: The evaluator must select Task A and at least one other Task.

Task A. Rapid Deceleration/Quick Stop

References: *FAA-H-8083-2, FAA-H-8083-4, FAA-H-8083-9, FAA-H-8083-21, FAA-H-8083-25; POH/RFM*

Objective: To determine the applicant understands rapid deceleration/quick stop, can apply that knowledge, manage associated risks, demonstrate appropriate skills, and provide effective instruction.

Knowledge:	The applicant demonstrates instructional knowledge by describing and explaining:
HI.X.A.K1	Purpose of the maneuver.
HI.X.A.K2	Effects of atmospheric conditions on a rapid deceleration/quick stop.
HI.X.A.K3	Wind correction techniques during rapid deceleration/quick stop.
HI.X.A.K4	Common errors related to this Task.

Risk Management:	The applicant explains and teaches how to identify and manage risk associated with:
HI.X.A.R1	Recognition of the need for a rapid deceleration/quick stop.
HI.X.A.R2	Powerplant and rotor management.
HI.X.A.R3	Vortex ring state (VRS).
HI.X.A.R4	Collision hazards.
HI.X.A.R5	Distractions, task prioritization, loss of situational awareness, or disorientation.

Skills:	The applicant demonstrates and simultaneously explains how to:
HI.X.A.S1	Complete the appropriate checklist(s).
HI.X.A.S2	Maintain powerplant and main rotor (Nr) speed within normal limits.
HI.X.A.S3	Coordinate all controls throughout the execution of the maneuver to terminate in a hover at an appropriate hover height.
HI.X.A.S4	Maintain an altitude that permits safe clearance between the tail boom and the surface.
HI.X.A.S5	Maintain heading throughout the maneuver, ±5°.
HI.X.A.S6	Analyze and correct common errors related to this Task.

Task B. Straight-In Autorotation in a Single-Engine Helicopter

References: *AC 61-65, AC 61-140; FAA-H-8083-2, FAA-H-8083-4, FAA-H-8083-9, FAA-H-8083-21, FAA-H-8083-25; POH/RFM*

Objective: To determine the applicant understands straight-in autorotation in a single engine helicopter, can apply that knowledge, manage associated risks, demonstrate appropriate skills, and provide effective instruction.

Note: *See Appendix 2: Safety of Flight and Appendix 3: Aircraft, Equipment, and Operational Requirements & Limitations for information related to this Task.*

Knowledge:	The applicant demonstrates instructional knowledge by describing and explaining:
HI.X.B.K1	Elements related to straight-in autorotation.

HI.X.B.K2	Effects of wind, weight, temperature, and density altitude.
HI.X.B.K3	Main rotor (Nr) speed.
HI.X.B.K4	Energy management.
HI.X.B.K5	Causes and effects of high descent rates.
HI.X.B.K6	Effect of varying bank angles, airspeeds, and rotor rpm.
HI.X.B.K7	Common errors related to this Task.

Risk Management: The applicant explains and teaches how to identify and manage risk associated with:

HI.X.B.R1	Low entry altitudes.
HI.X.B.R2	Flight control inputs.
HI.X.B.R3	Turbulence, including wake turbulence.
HI.X.B.R4	Windshear.
HI.X.B.R5	Exchange of flight controls during an intervention.
HI.X.B.R6	Main rotor (Nr) speed.
HI.X.B.R7	Energy management.
HI.X.B.R8	Low rotor rpm or rotor stall.
HI.X.B.R9	Main rotor (Nr) overspeed.
HI.X.B.R10	Excessive rate of descent.
HI.X.B.R11	Powerplant failure during the maneuver.
HI.X.B.R12	Collision hazards.
HI.X.B.R13	Terminating an autorotation.
HI.X.B.R14	Power recovery and go-around.
HI.X.B.R15	Distractions, task prioritization, loss of situational awareness, or disorientation.

Skills: The applicant demonstrates and simultaneously explains how to:

HI.X.B.S1	Complete the appropriate checklist(s).
HI.X.B.S2	Make radio calls as appropriate.
HI.X.B.S3	Select a suitable landing area.
HI.X.B.S4	Clear the area.
HI.X.B.S5	Select an appropriate entry altitude.
HI.X.B.S6	Initiate the maneuver at the proper point.
HI.X.B.S7	Establish power-off glide with the helicopter trimmed and autorotation airspeed, ±5 knots.
HI.X.B.S8	Maintain main rotor (Nr) within normal limits.
HI.X.B.S9	Compensate for wind speed and direction as necessary to avoid undershooting or overshooting the selected landing area.
HI.X.B.S10	Use proper deceleration and collective pitch application that permits safe clearance between the aircraft tail boom and the surface.
HI.X.B.S11	Initiate proper power recovery, or touchdown to the surface as briefed by the evaluator.

HI.X.B.S12	Terminate autorotation to a stabilized hover, or to the surface within 100 feet of a designated point.
HI.X.B.S13	Analyze and correct common errors related to this Task.

Task C. Autorotation with Turns in a Single-Engine Helicopter

References: *AC 61-65, AC 61-140; FAA-H-8083-2, FAA-H-8083-4, FAA-H-8083-9, FAA-H-8083-21, FAA-H-8083-25; POH/RFM*

Objective: To determine the applicant understands autorotation with turns with a power recovery or touchdown to the surface, can apply that knowledge, manage associated risks, demonstrate appropriate skills, and provide effective instruction.

Note: *See Appendix 2: Safety of Flight and Appendix 3: Aircraft, Equipment, and Operational Requirements & Limitations for information related to this Task.*

Knowledge:	The applicant demonstrates instructional knowledge by describing and explaining:
HI.X.C.K1	Elements related to autorotation with turns.
HI.X.C.K2	Effects of wind, weight, temperature, and density altitude.
HI.X.C.K3	Various rotor systems and their effects on autorotation.
HI.X.C.K4	Main rotor (Nr) speed.
HI.X.C.K5	Energy management.
HI.X.C.K6	Causes and effects of high descent rates.
HI.X.C.K7	Effect of varying bank angles, airspeeds, and rotor rpm.
HI.X.C.K8	Common errors related to this Task.

Risk Management:	The applicant explains and teaches how to identify and manage risk associated with:
HI.X.C.R1	Low entry altitudes.
HI.X.C.R2	Flight control inputs.
HI.X.C.R3	Turbulence, including wake turbulence.
HI.X.C.R4	Windshear.
HI.X.C.R5	Energy management.
HI.X.C.R6	Main rotor (Nr) speed.
HI.X.C.R7	Low rotor rpm or rotor stall.
HI.X.C.R8	Excessive rate of descent.
HI.X.C.R9	Powerplant failure during the maneuver.
HI.X.C.R10	Rolling out of the turn.
HI.X.C.R11	Collision hazards.
HI.X.C.R12	Terminating an autorotation.
HI.X.C.R13	Power recovery and go-around.
HI.X.C.R14	Distractions, task prioritization, loss of situational awareness, or disorientation.

Skills: The applicant demonstrates and simultaneously explains how to:

HI.X.C.S1	Complete the appropriate checklist(s).
HI.X.C.S2	Make radio calls as appropriate.
HI.X.C.S3	Select a suitable landing area.
HI.X.C.S4	Clear the area.
HI.X.C.S5	Select an appropriate entry altitude.
HI.X.C.S6	Initiate the maneuver at the proper point.
HI.X.C.S7	Establish power-off glide with the aircraft properly trimmed and autorotation airspeed, ±5 knots.
HI.X.C.S8	Maintain main rotor (Nr) within normal limits.
HI.X.C.S9	Maneuver to avoid undershooting or overshooting the selected landing area.
HI.X.C.S10	Roll out no lower than 300 feet above ground level (AGL) along the flight path to the selected landing area.
HI.X.C.S12	Use proper deceleration and collective pitch application that permits safe clearance between the aircraft tail boom and the surface.
HI.X.C.S13	Initiate proper power recovery, or touchdown to the surface as briefed by the evaluator.
HI.X.C.S14	Terminate autorotation to a stabilized hover, or to the surface within 100 feet of a designated point.
HI.X.C.S15	Analyze and correct common errors related to this Task.

Area of Operation XI. Emergency Operations

Note: *The evaluator must test at least one Task from Tasks A through G. The evaluator must also select at least one Task from Tasks H through M, which are tested orally only.*

Task A. Powerplant Failure in a Hover in a Single-Engine Helicopter

References: *FAA-H-8083-2, FAA-H-8083-4, FAA-H-8083-9, FAA-H-8083-21, FAA-H-8083-25; POH/RFM*

Objective: To determine the applicant understands power failure in a ground effect hover, can apply that knowledge, manage associated risks, demonstrate appropriate skills, and provide effective instruction.

Note: *See Appendix 2: Safety of Flight.*

Knowledge:	The applicant demonstrates instructional knowledge by describing and explaining:
HI.XI.A.K1	Elements related to powerplant failure in a hover, including energy management concepts.
HI.XI.A.K2	Effects of wind, weight, temperature, and density altitude.
HI.XI.A.K3	High and low inertia of rotor systems.
HI.XI.A.K4	Aerodynamics associated with powerplant failure in a hover.
HI.XI.A.K5	Proper orientation, division of attention, and proper planning.
HI.XI.A.K6	Common errors related to this Task.

Risk Management:	The applicant explains and teaches how to identify and manage risk associated with:
HI.XI.A.R1	Powerplant failure in a hover.
HI.XI.A.R2	Flight control inputs.
HI.XI.A.R3	Helicopter movement.
HI.XI.A.R4	Dynamic rollover.
HI.XI.A.R5	Distractions, task prioritization, loss of situational awareness, or disorientation.

Skills:	The applicant demonstrates and simultaneously explains how to:
HI.XI.A.S1	Complete the appropriate checklist(s).
HI.XI.A.S2	Make radio calls as appropriate.
HI.XI.A.S3	Clear the area.
HI.XI.A.S4	Select a suitable landing area.
HI.XI.A.S5	Establish a stationary or forward hover into the wind.
HI.XI.A.S6	Simulate powerplant failure.
HI.XI.A.S7	Maintain a heading, ±5°, throughout the maneuver.
HI.XI.A.S8	Touchdown with minimum sideward movement and no rearward movement.
HI.XI.A.S9	Use appropriate flight control inputs to cushion the touchdown.
HI.XI.A.S10	After touchdown, lower collective and neutralize flight controls.
HI.XI.A.S11	Analyze and correct common errors related to this Task.

Task B. Powerplant Failure at Altitude in a Single-Engine Helicopter

References: AC 61-140; FAA-H-8083-2, FAA-H-8083-4, FAA-H-8083-9, FAA-H-8083-21, FAA-H-8083-25; POH/RFM

Objective: To determine the applicant understands power failure at altitude, can apply that knowledge, manage associated risks, demonstrate appropriate skills, and provide effective instruction.

Note: See Appendix 2: Safety of Flight and Appendix 3: Aircraft, Equipment, and Operational Requirements & Limitations for information related to this Task.

Knowledge: The applicant demonstrates instructional knowledge by describing and explaining:

HI.XI.B.K1	Elements of a powerplant failure at altitude.
HI.XI.B.K2	Main rotor (Nr) speed.
HI.XI.B.K3	Effects of wind, weight, temperature, and density altitude.
HI.XI.B.K4	Energy management.
HI.XI.B.K5	Causes and effects of high descent rates.
HI.XI.B.K6	Effect of varying bank angles, airspeeds, and rotor rpm.
HI.XI.B.K7	Common errors related to this Task.

Risk Management: The applicant explains and teaches how to identify and manage risk associated with:

HI.XI.B.R1	Low entry altitudes.
HI.XI.B.R2	Selection of landing area.
HI.XI.B.R3	Flight control inputs.
HI.XI.B.R4	Turbulence, including wake turbulence.
HI.XI.B.R5	Windshear.
HI.XI.B.R6	Low rotor rpm or rotor stall.
HI.XI.B.R7	Powerplant failure during the maneuver.
HI.XI.B.R8	Collision hazards.
HI.XI.B.R9	Autorotation power-off never-exceed speed (V_{NE}) limitation.
HI.XI.B.R10	Helicopter trim.
HI.XI.B.R11	Distractions, task prioritization, loss of situational awareness, or disorientation.

Skills: The applicant demonstrates and simultaneously explains how to:

HI.XI.B.S1	Establish an autorotation.
HI.XI.B.S2	Establish power-off glide with the helicopter trimmed and autorotation airspeed, ±5 knots.
HI.XI.B.S3	Maintain main rotor (Nr) within normal limits.
HI.XI.B.S4	Select a suitable landing area considering altitude, wind, terrain, and obstructions.
HI.XI.B.S5	Compensate for wind speed and direction as necessary to avoid undershooting or overshooting the selected landing area.
HI.XI.B.S6	Make radio calls as appropriate.
HI.XI.B.S7	Terminate approach with a power recovery at a safe altitude as directed by the evaluator.
HI.XI.B.S8	Analyze and correct common errors related to this Task.

Task C. Approach and Landing with One Engine Inoperative (OEI) (Simulated) (Multiengine Helicopter Only)

References: FAA-H-8083-2, FAA-H-8083-4, FAA-H-8083-9, FAA-H-8083-21, FAA-H-8083-25; POH/RFM

Objective: To determine the applicant understands approach and landing with one engine inoperative (OEI) (simulated), can apply that knowledge, manage associated risks, demonstrate appropriate skills, and provide effective instruction.

Note: See Appendix 2: Safety of Flight and Appendix 3: Aircraft, Equipment, and Operational Requirements & Limitations for information related to this Task.

Knowledge:	The applicant demonstrates instructional knowledge by describing and explaining:
HI.XI.C.K1	Elements of approach and landing with one engine inoperative.
HI.XI.C.K2	Effects of atmospheric conditions on emergency approach and landing.
HI.XI.C.K3	Stabilized approach.
HI.XI.C.K4	Approach and landing profiles and aircraft configuration.
HI.XI.C.K5	Common errors related to this Task.

Risk Management:	The applicant explains and teaches how to identify and manage risk associated with:
HI.XI.C.R1	Consideration of altitude, wind, terrain, obstructions, and available landing area.
HI.XI.C.R2	Planning and following a flightpath to the selected landing area.
HI.XI.C.R3	Collision hazards.
HI.XI.C.R4	Distractions, task prioritization, loss of situational awareness, or disorientation.

Skills:	The applicant demonstrates and simultaneously explains how to:
HI.XI.C.S1	Maintain the operating powerplant within OEI limits.
HI.XI.C.S2	Maintain, prior to beginning the final approach segment, the recommended flight profile with altitude ±100 feet, airspeed, ±10 knots, heading ±5°, and maintains track.
HI.XI.C.S3	Make radio calls as appropriate.
HI.XI.C.S4	Plan and follow a flightpath to the selected landing area considering altitude, wind, terrain, and obstructions.
HI.XI.C.S5	Complete the appropriate checklist(s).
HI.XI.C.S6	Maintain directional control and appropriate crosswind correction throughout the approach and landing.
HI.XI.C.S7	Use single-pilot resource management (SRM) or crew resource management (CRM), as appropriate.
HI.XI.C.S8	Analyze and correct common errors related to this Task.

Task D. Flight Solely by Reference to Instruments

References: 14 CFR part 61; FAA-H-8083-2, FAA-H-8083-4, FAA-8083-9, FAA-H-8083-15, FAA-H-8083-21, FAA-H-8083-25

Objective: To determine the applicant understands attitude instrument flying, can apply that knowledge, manage associated risks, demonstrate appropriate skills, and provide effective instruction, solely by reference to instruments.

Knowledge:	The applicant demonstrates instructional knowledge by describing and explaining:
HI.XI.D.K1	Elements related to attitude instrument flying during straight-and-level flight, climbs, turns, and descents.
HI.XI.D.K2	Interpretation, operation, and limitations of pitch, bank, and power instruments.
HI.XI.D.K3	Normal and abnormal instrument indications and operations.
HI.XI.D.K4	Common errors related to this Task.

Risk Management:	The applicant explains and teaches how to identify and manage risk associated with:
HI.XI.D.R1	Situations that can affect physiology and degrade instrument cross-check.
HI.XI.D.R2	Spatial disorientation and optical illusions.
HI.XI.D.R3	Flying an unfamiliar aircraft, or operating with unfamiliar flight display systems and avionics.

Skills:	The applicant demonstrates and simultaneously explains how to:
HI.XI.D.S1	Maintain straight and level flight, altitude ±200 feet, heading ±20°, and airspeed ±10 knots.
HI.XI.D.S2	Make a constant airspeed climb, airspeed ±10 knots, in straight flight and turns to a heading ±20°, and level off and maintain assigned altitude ±200 feet.
HI.XI.D.S3	Make a constant airspeed descent, airspeed ±10 knots, in straight flight and turns to a heading ±20°, and level off and maintain assigned altitude ±200 feet.
HI.XI.D.S4	Use proper instrument cross-check and interpretation, and apply the appropriate pitch, bank, power, maintain coordinated flight throughout the maneuver.
HI.XI.D.S5	Demonstrate SRM/CRM.
HI.XI.D.S6	Analyze and correct common errors related to this Task.

Task E. Recovery from Unusual Flight Attitudes

References:	AIM; FAA-H-8083-2, FAA-H-8083-4, FAA-H-8083-9, FAA-H-8083-15, FAA-H-8083-21, FAA-H-8083-25; POH/RFM
Objective:	To determine the applicant understands attitude instrument flying while recovering from unusual attitudes, can apply that knowledge, manage associated risks, demonstrate appropriate skills, and provide effective instruction, solely by reference to instruments.
Note:	See Appendix 3: Aircraft, Equipment, and Operational Requirements & Limitations for information related to this Task.

Knowledge:	The applicant demonstrates instructional knowledge by describing and explaining:
HI.XI.E.K1	Prevention of unusual attitudes, including flight causal, physiological, and environmental factors, and system and equipment failures.
HI.XI.E.K2	Procedures for recovery from unusual attitudes in flight.
HI.XI.E.K3	Procedures available to safely regain visual meteorological conditions (VMC) after flight into inadvertent instrument meteorological conditions or unintended instrument meteorological conditions (IIMC)/(UIMC).
HI.XI.E.K4	Appropriate use of automation, if applicable.
HI.XI.E.K5	Common errors related to this Task.

Risk
Management: The applicant explains and teaches how to identify and manage risk associated with:

HI.XI.E.R1   Situations that could lead to loss of control in-flight (LOC-I) or unusual attitudes in-flight (e.g., stress, task saturation, inadequate instrument scan distractions, and spatial disorientation).

HI.XI.E.R2   Assessment of the unusual attitude.

HI.XI.E.R3   Control input errors, inducing undesired aircraft attitudes.

HI.XI.E.R4   Collision hazards.

HI.XI.E.R5   Distractions, task prioritization, loss of situational awareness, or disorientation.

HI.XI.E.R6   Interpreting flight instruments.

HI.XI.E.R7   Control application solely by reference to instruments.

HI.XI.E.R8   Operating envelope considerations.

Skills: The applicant demonstrates and simultaneously explains how to:

HI.XI.E.S1   Use proper instrument cross-check and interpretation to identify an unusual attitude (including both nose-high and nose-low), and apply the appropriate pitch, bank, and power corrections, in the correct sequence, to return to a stabilized level flight attitude.

HI.XI.E.S2   Use single-pilot resource management (SRM) or crew resource management (CRM), as appropriate.

HI.XI.E.S3   Analyze and correct common errors related to this Task.

Task F. Vortex Ring State (VRS)

References: FAA-H-8083-2, FAA-H-8083-4, FAA-H-8083-9, FAA-H-8083-21, FAA-H-8083-25; POH/RFM

Objective: To determine the applicant understands Vortex Ring State (VRS), can apply that knowledge, manage associated risks, demonstrate appropriate skills, and provide effective instruction.

Note: See Appendix 3: Aircraft, Equipment, and Operational Requirements & Limitations for information related to this Task.

Knowledge: The applicant demonstrates instructional knowledge by describing and explaining:

HI.XI.F.K1   Elements of vortex ring state.

HI.XI.F.K2   Effects of wind, weight, temperature, and density altitude.

HI.XI.F.K3   Requirements for the formation of VRS.

HI.XI.F.K4   Aerodynamics and indications of VRS.

HI.XI.F.K5   Flight scenarios under which VRS can occur.

HI.XI.F.K6   Effective recovery techniques.

HI.XI.F.K7   Common errors related to this Task.

Risk
Management: The applicant explains and teaches how to identify and manage risk associated with:

HI.XI.F.R1   Pilot recognition and response to VRS.

HI.XI.F.R2   Entering the maneuver at a lower altitude than planned.

HI.XI.F.R3   Collision hazards.

HI.XI.F.R4	Distractions, task prioritization, loss of situational awareness, or disorientation.
HI.XI.F.R5	Application of power or exceeding powerplant limitations.
HI.XI.F.R6	Loss of tail rotor effectiveness (LTE).

Skills:	The applicant demonstrates and simultaneously explains how to:
HI.XI.F.S1	Complete the appropriate checklist(s).
HI.XI.F.S2	Clear the area.
HI.XI.F.S3	Select an altitude that allows recovery to be completed no lower than 1,000 feet AGL or as recommended by the manufacturer, whichever is higher.
HI.XI.F.S4	Establish conditions leading to VRS entry.
HI.XI.F.S5	Promptly recognize, announce, and recover at the first indication of VRS.
HI.XI.F.S6	Use single-pilot resource management (SRM) or crew resource management (CRM), as appropriate.
HI.XI.F.S7	Analyze and correct common errors related to this Task.

Task G. Low Rotor Revolutions Per Minute (RPM) Recognition and Recovery

References: FAA-H-8083-2, FAA-H-8083-4, FAA-H-8083-9, FAA-H-8083-21, FAA-H-8083-25; POH/RFM

Objective: To determine the applicant understands low rotor rpm recognition and recovery, can apply that knowledge, manage associated risks, demonstrate appropriate skills, and provide effective instruction.

Note: See Appendix 3: Aircraft, Equipment, and Operational Requirements & Limitations for information related to this Task.

Knowledge:	The applicant demonstrates instructional knowledge by describing and explaining:
HI.XI.G.K1	Elements related to low rotor rpm recovery energy management, including the combination of conditions that may lead to this situation.
HI.XI.G.K2	Effects of wind, weight, temperature, and density altitude.
HI.XI.G.K3	Aerodynamics that affect low rotor rpm conditions.
HI.XI.G.K4	Powerplant performance.
HI.XI.G.K5	Main rotor (Nr) limitations.
HI.XI.G.K6	Difference between low rotor rpm and blade stall.
HI.XI.G.K7	Common errors related to this Task.

Risk Management:	The applicant explains and teaches how to identify and manage risk associated with:
HI.XI.G.R1	Powerplant limitations.
HI.XI.G.R2	Powerplant governor operation.
HI.XI.G.R3	Collision hazards.
HI.XI.G.R4	Distractions, task prioritization, loss of situational awareness, or disorientation.
HI.XI.G.R5	Low inertia rotor systems.

Skills:	The applicant demonstrates and simultaneously explains how to:
HI.XI.G.S1	Complete the appropriate checklist(s).
HI.XI.G.S2	Clear the area.
HI.XI.G.S3	Detect the development of low rotor rpm and initiate prompt corrective action.
HI.XI.G.S4	Execute the recovery procedure to return rotor rpm to normal limits.
HI.XI.G.S5	Analyze and correct common errors related to this Task.

Task H. Systems and Equipment Malfunctions

References: FAA-H-8083-2, FAA-H-8083-4, FAA-H-8083-9, FAA-H-8083-21, FAA-H-8083-25; POH/RFM

Objective: To determine the applicant understands system and equipment malfunctions appropriate to the aircraft provided for the practical test, can apply that knowledge, manage associated risks, demonstrate appropriate skills, and provide effective instruction.

Knowledge:	The applicant demonstrates instructional knowledge by describing and explaining:
HI.XI.H.K1	Causes of partial or complete power loss related to the specific type of powerplant(s).
HI.XI.H.K2	System and equipment malfunctions specific to the helicopter, including:
HI.XI.H.K2a	a. Electrical malfunction
HI.XI.H.K2b	b. Flight instrument malfunctions
HI.XI.H.K2c	c. Pitot-static system malfunction
HI.XI.H.K2d	d. Electronic flight instrument display malfunction
HI.XI.H.K2e	e. Landing gear malfunctions
HI.XI.H.K2f	f. Inoperative flight control/trim
HI.XI.H.K2g	g. Hydraulic failure, if applicable
HI.XI.H.K3	Various frequency vibrations and the possible components that may be affected.
HI.XI.H.K4	Causes and remedies for smoke or fire onboard the aircraft.
HI.XI.H.K5	Any other system malfunction specific to the helicopter flown.
HI.XI.H.K6	Common errors related to this Task.

Risk Management:	The applicant explains and teaches how to identify and manage risk associated with:
HI.XI.H.R1	Startle response.
HI.XI.H.R2	Checklist usage for a system or equipment malfunction.
HI.XI.H.R3	Distractions, task prioritization, loss of situational awareness, or disorientation.
HI.XI.H.R4	Undesired aircraft state.

Skills:	The applicant demonstrates and simultaneously explains how to:
HI.XI.H.S1	Determine appropriate action for simulated emergencies specified by the evaluator, from at least four of the elements or sub-elements listed in K1 through K5.
HI.XI.H.S2	Complete the appropriate checklist(s).
HI.XI.H.S3	Analyze and correct common errors related to this Task.

Task I. Dynamic Rollover

References: FAA-H-8083-2, FAA-H-8083-4, FAA-H-8083-9, FAA-H-8083-21, FAA-H-8083-25; POH/RFM; SAFO 16016

Objective: To determine the applicant understands dynamic rollover, can apply that knowledge, manage associated risks, demonstrate appropriate skills, and provide effective instruction.

Note: Evaluator assesses this Task orally only.

Knowledge:	The applicant demonstrates instructional knowledge by describing and explaining:
HI.XI.I.K1	Elements related to dynamic rollover.
HI.XI.I.K2	Interactions between thrust, crosswind, slope, lateral CG, aircraft weight, and flight controls that contribute to dynamic rollover.
HI.XI.I.K3	Preventive flight technique and recovery during flight operations, including slope operations.
HI.XI.I.K4	Common errors related to this Task.

Risk Management:	The applicant explains and teaches how to identify and manage risk associated with:
HI.XI.I.R1	Surface conditions conducive to dynamic rollover.
HI.XI.I.R2	Landing gear proximity to obstructions on the ground during low altitude hover.
HI.XI.I.R3	Flight control inputs during takeoff or landing.
HI.XI.I.R4	Sideward hover.
HI.XI.I.R5	Aircraft slope limitations.
HI.XI.I.R6	Critical rollover angle and rolling moment.
HI.XI.I.R7	Translating tendency.

Skills:	The applicant demonstrates and simultaneously explains how to:
HI.XI.I.S1	[Intentionally left blank].

Task J. Ground Resonance

References: FAA-H-8083-2, FAA-H-8083-4, FAA-H-8083-9, FAA-H-8083-21, FAA-H-8083-25; POH/RFM

Objective: To determine the applicant understands ground resonance, can apply that knowledge, manage associated risks, demonstrate appropriate skills, and provide effective instruction.

Note: Evaluator assesses this Task orally only.

Knowledge:	The applicant demonstrates instructional knowledge by describing and explaining:
HI.XI.J.K1	Exhibits knowledge of the elements related to ground resonance by describing:
HI.XI.J.K1a	a. Conditions that contribute to ground resonance
HI.XI.J.K1b	b. Preventive flight technique during takeoffs and landings
HI.XI.J.K1c	c. Landing surface
HI.XI.J.K2	Inspection of items that may contribute to ground resonance.
HI.XI.J.K3	Corrective actions during low and normal rotor rpm speeds.
HI.XI.J.K4	Common errors related to this Task.

Risk
Management: The applicant explains and teaches how to identify and manage risk associated with:

HI.XI.J.R1   Factors that may contribute to the onset of ground resonance.

HI.XI.J.R2   Recognition of the onset of ground resonance.

HI.XI.J.R3   Recovery procedure selection.

Skills: The applicant demonstrates and simultaneously explains how to:

HI.XI.J.S1   [Intentionally left blank].

Task K. Low Gravity (G) Recognition and Recovery

References: *FAA-H-8083-2, FAA-H-8083-4, FAA-H-8083-9, FAA-H-8083-21, FAA-H-8083-25; POH/RFM*

Objective: To determine the applicant understands low G recognition and recovery, can apply that knowledge, manage associated risks, demonstrate appropriate skills, and provide effective instruction.

Note: *Evaluator assesses this Task orally only.*

Knowledge: The applicant demonstrates instructional knowledge by describing and explaining:

HI.XI.K.K1   Exhibits knowledge of the elements related to low G conditions by describing:

HI.XI.K.K1a   a. Aerodynamic factors related to low G conditions

HI.XI.K.K1b   b. Situations that contribute to low G conditions

HI.XI.K.K1c   c. Avoidance, recognition, and appropriate recovery procedures

HI.XI.K.K2   Effects of low G conditions on various rotor systems.

HI.XI.K.K3   Pilot responses that lead to mast bumping in a low G condition, if applicable.

HI.XI.K.K4   Common errors related to this Task.

Risk
Management: The applicant explains and teaches how to identify and manage risk associated with:

HI.XI.K.R1   Control inputs that cause low G conditions.

HI.XI.K.R2   Turbulence/gusty wind conditions.

HI.XI.K.R3   Control inputs that cause mast bumping.

Skills: The applicant demonstrates and simultaneously explains how to:

HI.XI.K.S1   [Intentionally left blank].

Task L. Emergency Equipment and Survival Gear

References: *AC 61-65; FAA-H-8083-2, FAA-H-8083-4, FAA-H-8083-9, FAA-H-8083-21, FAA-H-8083-25; POH/RFM*

Objective: To determine the applicant understands emergency equipment and survival gear, can apply that knowledge, manage associated risks, demonstrate appropriate skills, and provide effective instruction.

Knowledge: The applicant demonstrates instructional knowledge by describing and explaining:

HI.XI.L.K1 Emergency Locator Transmitter (ELT) operations, limitations, and testing requirements.

HI.XI.L.K2 Fire extinguisher operations and limitations.

HI.XI.L.K3 Emergency equipment and survival gear needed for:

HI.XI.L.K3a a. Climate extremes (hot/cold)

HI.XI.L.K3b b. Mountainous terrain

HI.XI.L.K3c c. Overwater operations

HI.XI.L.K4 Common errors related to this Task.

Risk Management: The applicant explains and teaches how to identify and manage risk associated with:

HI.XI.L.R1 Survival gear (water, clothing, shelter) for 48 to 72 hours.

Skills: The applicant demonstrates and simultaneously explains how to:

HI.XI.L.S1 Identify appropriate equipment and personal gear.

HI.XI.L.S2 Brief passengers on proper use of on-board emergency equipment and survival gear.

HI.XI.L.S3 Analyze and correct common errors related to this Task.

Task M. Antitorque System Failure

References: FAA-H-8083-2, FAA-H-8083-4, FAA-H-8083-9, FAA-H-8083-21, FAA-H-8083-25; POH/RFM

Objective: To determine the applicant understands antitorque system failure, can apply that knowledge, manage associated risks, demonstrate appropriate skills, and provide effective instruction.

Note: Evaluator assesses this Task orally only.

Knowledge: The applicant demonstrates instructional knowledge by describing and explaining:

HI.XI.M.K1 Elements related to antitorque system failure by describing:

HI.XI.M.K1a a. Indications of an antitorque system failure(s)

HI.XI.M.K1b b. Differences between complete loss of antitorque and mechanical flight control failures

HI.XI.M.K1c c. RFM procedures for antitorque system(s) failure

HI.XI.M.K2 Wind conditions that favor a landing with an antitorque failure.

HI.XI.M.K3 Common errors related to this Task.

Risk Management: The applicant explains and teaches how to identify and manage risk associated with:

HI.XI.M.R1 Preflight inspection of the antitorque system.

HI.XI.M.R2 Antitorque failure(s) for the aircraft supplied for the practical test.

HI.XI.M.R3 Use of antitorque failure procedures.

Skills: The applicant demonstrates and simultaneously explains how to:

HI.XI.M.S1 [Intentionally left blank].

Area of Operation XII. Special Operations

Note: *The evaluator must select at least one Task from this Area of Operation.*

Task A. Confined Area Operations

References: *FAA-H-8083-2, FAA-H-8083-4, FAA-H-8083-9, FAA-H-8083-21, FAA-H-8083-25; POH/RFM*

Objective: To determine the applicant understands confined area operation, can apply that knowledge, manage associated risks, demonstrate appropriate skills, and provide effective instruction.

Knowledge:	The applicant demonstrates instructional knowledge by describing and explaining:
HI.XII.A.K1	Elements of confined area operations.
HI.XII.A.K2	Effects of wind, weight, temperature, and density altitude.
HI.XII.A.K3	Situations when a confined area approach and landing is recommended and factors related to landing performance including H/V diagram information.
HI.XII.A.K4	High and low reconnaissance, including takeoff and departure planning.
HI.XII.A.K5	Power requirements versus power available for the departure or arrival profile(s).
HI.XII.A.K6	Common errors related to this Task.

Risk Management:	The applicant explains and teaches how to identify and manage risk associated with:
HI.XII.A.R1	Selection of approach path, termination point and departure path based on aircraft performance and limitations, wind, and availability of alternate sites.
HI.XII.A.R2	Effects of:
HI.XII.A.R2a	a. Wind Direction
HI.XII.A.R2b	b. Windshear
HI.XII.A.R2c	c. Turbulence
HI.XII.A.R3	H/V diagram information.
HI.XII.A.R4	Go-around.
HI.XII.A.R5	Forced landing during the maneuver.
HI.XII.A.R6	Landing surface.
HI.XII.A.R7	Dynamic rollover.
HI.XII.A.R8	Ground resonance.
HI.XII.A.R9	Low rotor rpm.
HI.XII.A.R10	Loss of tail rotor effectiveness (LTE).
HI.XII.A.R11	Collision hazards.
HI.XII.A.R12	Vortex ring state (VRS).
HI.XII.A.R13	Aircraft limitations.
HI.XII.A.R14	Distractions, task prioritization, loss of situational awareness, or disorientation.
HI.XII.A.R15	Power requirements versus power available for the departure or arrival profile(s).

Skills:	The applicant demonstrates and simultaneously explains how to:
HI.XII.A.S1	Complete the appropriate checklist(s).

HI.XII.A.S2	Make radio calls as appropriate.
HI.XII.A.S3	Confirm power available meets or exceeds the power required for the selected arrival or departure profile(s).
HI.XII.A.S4	Determine wind direction with or without visible wind direction indicators.
HI.XII.A.S5	Accomplish a proper high and low reconnaissance of the confined landing area.
HI.XII.A.S6	Select a suitable approach path, termination point, and departure path.
HI.XII.A.S7	Track the selected approach path at an acceptable approach angle and rate of closure to the termination point.
HI.XII.A.S8	Continually evaluate the suitability of the confined landing area and termination point.
HI.XII.A.S9	Maintain powerplant and main rotor (Nr) speed within normal limits.
HI.XII.A.S10	Accomplish a proper ground reconnaissance.
HI.XII.A.S11	Terminate in a hover or on the surface, as appropriate.
HI.XII.A.S12	Select a suitable takeoff point, considers factors affecting takeoff and climb performance under various conditions.
HI.XII.A.S13	Use single-pilot resource management (SRM) or crew resource management (CRM), as appropriate.
HI.XII.A.S14	Analyze and correct common errors related to this Task.

Task B. Pinnacle Operations

References: FAA-H-8083-2, FAA-H-8083-4, FAA-H-8083-9, FAA-H-8083-21, FAA-H-8083-25; POH/RFM

Objective: To determine the applicant understands pinnacle operations, can apply that knowledge, manage associated risks, demonstrate appropriate skills, and provide effective instruction.

Knowledge:	The applicant demonstrates instructional knowledge by describing and explaining:
HI.XII.B.K1	Elements of pinnacle/platform operations.
HI.XII.B.K2	Effects of wind, weight, temperature, and density altitude.
HI.XII.B.K3	Suitable takeoff point and departure flight path during climb.
HI.XII.B.K4	Situations when a pinnacle/platform approach, landing and takeoff is recommended and factors related to aircraft performance.
HI.XII.B.K5	Elements of a high and low reconnaissance.
HI.XII.B.K6	Common errors related to this Task.

Risk Management:	The applicant explains and teaches how to identify and manage risk associated with:
HI.XII.B.R1	Selection of approach path, termination point and departure path based on aircraft performance and limitations, and wind.
HI.XII.B.R2	Effects of:
HI.XII.B.R2a	a. Wind Direction
HI.XII.B.R2b	b. Windshear
HI.XII.B.R2c	c. Turbulence
HI.XII.B.R3	H/V diagram information.

HI.XII.B.R4	Go-around.
HI.XII.B.R5	Powerplant failure during approach/landing phase of flight.
HI.XII.B.R6	Collision hazards.
HI.XII.B.R7	Vortex ring state (VRS).
HI.XII.B.R8	Landing surface.
HI.XII.B.R9	Low rotor rpm.
HI.XII.B.R10	Dynamic rollover.
HI.XII.B.R11	Ground resonance.
HI.XII.B.R12	Loss of tail rotor effectiveness (LTE).
HI.XII.B.R13	Aircraft limitations.
HI.XII.B.R14	Distractions, task prioritization, loss of situational awareness, or disorientation.
HI.XII.B.R15	Forced landing.
HI.XII.B.R16	Main and tail rotor hazards for passengers.

Skills:	The applicant demonstrates and simultaneously explains how to:
HI.XII.B.S1	Complete the appropriate checklist(s).
HI.XII.B.S2	Confirm power available meets or exceeds the power required for the selected arrival or departure profile(s).
HI.XII.B.S3	Make radio calls as appropriate.
HI.XII.B.S4	Accomplish high and low reconnaissance.
HI.XII.B.S5	Determine wind direction with or without visible wind direction indicators.
HI.XII.B.S6	Select a suitable approach path, termination point, and departure path.
HI.XII.B.S7	Select an approach path considering wind direction.
HI.XII.B.S8	Track the selected approach path at an acceptable approach angle and rate of closure to the termination point.
HI.XII.B.S9	Maintain powerplant and main rotor (Nr) speed within normal limits.
HI.XII.B.S10	Accomplish a proper ground reconnaissance.
HI.XII.B.S11	Terminate in a hover or on the surface, as appropriate.
HI.XII.B.S12	Select a suitable takeoff point and consider factors affecting takeoff and climb performance under various conditions.
HI.XII.B.S13	Analyze and correct common errors related to this Task.

Area of Operation XIII. Postflight Procedures

Task A. After Landing, Parking, and Securing

References: FAA-H-8083-2, FAA-H-8083-4, FAA-H-8083-9, FAA-H-8083-21, FAA-H-8083-25; POH/RFM

Objective: To determine the applicant understands after landing, parking, and securing procedures, can apply that knowledge, manage associated risks, demonstrate appropriate skills, and provide effective instruction.

Knowledge:	The applicant demonstrates instructional knowledge by describing and explaining:
HI.XIII.A.K1	Helicopter shutdown, securing, and postflight inspection.
HI.XIII.A.K2	Documenting in-flight/postflight discrepancies.
HI.XIII.A.K3	Common errors related to this Task.

Risk Management:	The applicant explains and teaches how to identify and manage risk associated with:
HI.XIII.A.R1	Activities and distractions.
HI.XIII.A.R2	Parking the helicopter in a congested area.
HI.XIII.A.R3	Airport specific security procedures.
HI.XIII.A.R4	Disembarking passengers safely on the ramp and monitoring passenger movement while on the ramp.

Skills:	The applicant demonstrates and simultaneously explains how to:
HI.XIII.A.S1	Minimize the hazardous effects of rotor downwash during hovering.
HI.XIII.A.S2	Park in an appropriate area, considering the safety of nearby persons and property.
HI.XIII.A.S3	Complete the appropriate checklist(s).
HI.XIII.A.S5	Conduct a postflight inspection and document discrepancies and servicing requirements, if any.
HI.XIII.A.S6	Secure the helicopter.
HI.XIII.A.S7	Analyze and correct common errors related to this Task.

Appendix 1: Practical Test Roles, Responsibilities, and Outcomes

Eligibility Requirements for a Flight Instructor Pilot Certificate

The prerequisite requirements and general eligibility for a practical test and the specific requirements for the issuance of a Flight Instructor Certificate in the Rotorcraft Category Helicopter Rating can be found in 14 CFR part 61, sections 61.39(a) and 61.183.

In accordance with 14 CFR part 61, section 61.39, the applicant must pass the airman knowledge test before taking the practical test, if applicable to the certificate or rating sought.

For an initial flight instructor certificate or when adding the Rotorcraft Category Helicopter Rating to an existing flight instructor certificate, applicants must pass the applicable knowledge test(s) listed in the table below as a prerequisite for the practical test.

Test Code	Test Name	Number of Questions	Age	Allotted Time	Passing Score
FOI*	Fundamentals of Instructing	50	16	1.5	70
FRH	Flight Instructor Helicopter	100	16	2.5	70
HFA	Flight Instructor Helicopter (Added Rating)	25	16	1.0	70

*The FOI knowledge test applies unless the applicant meets the criteria listed in 14 CFR part 61, section 61.183(e).

Use of the ACS During a Practical Test

The practical test is conducted in accordance with the ACS and FAA regulations that are current as of the date of the test.

The Areas of Operation in this ACS align with the Areas of Operation found in 14 CFR part 61, section 61.187(b). Each Area of Operation includes Tasks appropriate to that Area of Operation. Each Task contains an Objective stating what the applicant must know, consider, and/or do. The ACS then lists the aeronautical knowledge, risk management, and skill elements relevant to the specific Task, along with the conditions and standards for acceptable performance. The ACS uses Notes to emphasize special considerations.

During the ground and flight portion of the practical test, the FAA expects evaluators to assess the applicant's mastery of the topic in accordance with the level of learning most appropriate for the specified Task. The oral questioning will continue throughout the entire practical test. For some topics, the evaluator will ask the applicant to describe or explain. For other items, the evaluator will assess the applicant's understanding by providing a scenario that requires the applicant to appropriately apply and/or correlate knowledge, experience, and information to the circumstances of the given scenario. The flight portion of the practical test requires the applicant to demonstrate knowledge, risk management, flight proficiency, and operational skill in accordance with the ACS.

The elements within each Task in this ACS are coded according to a scheme that includes four components. For example,

FI.I.C.K2:

    FI = Applicable ACS

    I = Area of Operation

    C = Task

    K2 = Task element (in this example, Knowledge 2)

There is no requirement for an evaluator to test every knowledge and risk management element in a Task; rather the evaluator has discretion to sample as needed to ensure the applicant's mastery of that Task. The required minimum elements to be tested from each applicable Task include:

- any elements in which the applicant was shown to be deficient on the knowledge test, as applicable;
- at least one knowledge element;
- at least one risk management element; and
- all skill elements unless otherwise noted.

The Airman Knowledge Test Report (AKTR) lists ACS codes that correlate to a specific Task element for a given Area of Operation for any incorrect responses on the knowledge test.

Knowledge and risk management elements are primarily evaluated during the knowledge testing phase of the airman certification process. The evaluator administering the practical test has the discretion to combine Tasks/elements as appropriate to testing scenarios.

Unless otherwise noted in the Task, the evaluator must test each item in the skills section by observing the applicant perform each one. As safety of flight conditions permit, the evaluator should use questions during flight to test knowledge and risk management elements not evident in the demonstrated skills. To the greatest extent practicable, evaluators should test the applicant's ability to apply and correlate information and use rote questions only when they are appropriate for the material being tested.

If the Task includes a knowledge or risk element with sub-elements, the evaluator may choose the primary element and select at least one sub-element to satisfy the requirement. Selection of the sub-element satisfies the requirement for one element unless otherwise noted.

For example, an evaluator who chooses FI.I.F.K2 may select a sub-element such as FI.I.F.K2b to satisfy the requirement to select one knowledge element.

The References for each Task indicate the source material for Task elements. For example, in the Task element "Acceptable weather products and resources required for preflight planning, current and forecast weather for departure, en route, and arrival phases of flight such as:" (HI.III.C.K2), the applicant should be prepared for questions on any weather product presented in the references for that Task.

The FAA encourages applicants and instructors to use the ACS when preparing for the airman knowledge tests and practical tests. Evaluators must conduct the practical test in accordance with the current ACS and FAA regulations pursuant to 14 CFR part 61, section 61.43. If an applicant is entitled to credit for Areas of Operation previously passed as indicated on a Notice of Disapproval of Application or Letter of Discontinuance, evaluators shall use the ACS currently in effect on the date of the test.

The ground portion of the practical test allows the evaluator to determine whether the applicant is sufficiently prepared to advance to the flight portion of the practical test. The applicant must pass the ground portion of the practical test before beginning the flight portion. The oral questioning will continue throughout the entire practical test.

Instructor Responsibilities

The instructor trains and qualifies the applicant to meet the established standards for knowledge, risk management, and skill elements in all Tasks appropriate to the certificate and rating sought. The instructor should use this ACS and its references when preparing the applicant to take the practical test and when retraining the applicant to proficiency in any subject(s) missed on the knowledge test.

Evaluator Responsibilities

An evaluator includes the following:

- Aviation Safety Inspector (ASI);
- Pilot examiner (other than administrative pilot examiners);
- Training center evaluator (TCE);
- Chief instructor, assistant chief instructor, or check instructor of pilot school holding examining authority; or
- Instrument Flight Instructor (CFII) conducting an instrument proficiency check (IPC).

The evaluator who conducts the practical test verifies the applicant has met the aeronautical experience requirements specified for a certificate or rating before administering the test. During the practical test, the evaluator determines whether the applicant meets the established standards of aeronautical knowledge, risk management, and skills for the Tasks in the appropriate ACS.

The evaluator must develop a plan of action (POA) that includes all required Areas of Operation and Tasks and administer each practical test in English. The POA must include scenario(s) that evaluate as many of the required Areas of Operation and Tasks as possible. As a scenario unfolds during the test, the evaluator will introduce problems and simulate emergencies that test the applicant's ability. The evaluator has the discretion to modify the POA to accommodate unexpected situations as they arise or suspend and later resume a scenario to assess certain Tasks.

Prior to and throughout the evaluation, the evaluator ensures the applicant meets the FAA Aviation English Language Standard (AELS). An applicant must be able to communicate in English in a discernible and understandable manner with air traffic control (ATC), pilots, and others involved in preparing an aircraft for flight and operating an aircraft in flight. This communication may or may not involve radio communications. An applicant for an FAA certificate or rating issued in accordance with 14 CFR parts 61, 63, 65, or 107 who cannot hear or speak due to a medical deficiency may be eligible for an FAA certificate with specific operational limitations.

If the applicant's ability to meet the FAA AELS comes into question before starting the practical test, the evaluator will not begin the practical test. An evaluator other than an ASI will check the box, "Referred to FSO for Aviation English Language Standard Determination," located on the bottom of page 2 of the applicant's FAA Form 8710-1, Airman Certificate and/or Rating Application, or FAA Form 8710-11, Airman Certificate and/or Rating Application - Sport Pilot, as applicable. The evaluator will refer the applicant to the appropriate Flight Standards Office (FSO).

If the applicant's ability to meet the FAA AELS comes into question after the practical test begins, an evaluator who other than an ASI will discontinue the practical test and check the box, "Referred to FSO for Aviation English Language Standard Determination," on the application. The evaluator will also issue FAA Form 8060-5, Notice of Disapproval of Application, with the comment "Does Not Demonstrate FAA AELS" in addition to any unsatisfactory Task(s). The evaluator will refer the applicant to the appropriate FSO. ASIs conducting the practical test may assess an applicant's English language proficiency in accordance with FAA Order 8900.1.

In either case, the evaluator must complete and submit the application file through normal application procedures and evaluators other than an ASI notify the appropriate FSO of the referral.

If the ability of an FAA certificated airman comes into question prior to or during a required regulatory check (e.g., proficiency check) the evaluator other than an ASI will not continue the check or provide an endorsement indicating completion. The evaluator will refer the airman to the jurisdictional FAA field office for further determination of ability to meet the FAA AELS.

For additional information, reference AC 60-28, FAA English Language Standard for an FAA Certificate issued under 14 CFR parts 61, 63, 65, and 107, as amended.

The evaluator may direct an applicant to start or complete a Task from the ground or to a hover if the Task element provides an option.

The evaluator conducting the practical test must determine that the applicant meets acceptable standards of teaching ability in the selected Tasks. The evaluator makes this determination by confirming the applicant's:

- Ability to apply the fundamentals of instructing;
- Knowledge of and ability to teach the subject matter, procedures, and maneuvers covered in the Tasks;
- Ability to perform the Tasks at the level of a commercial pilot while giving effective flight instruction; and
- Ability to analyze and correct common errors related to the procedures and maneuvers covered in the Tasks.

During the flight portion of the practical test, the evaluator may act as a student during selected maneuvers. This gives the evaluator an opportunity to evaluate the flight instructor applicant's ability to analyze and correct simulated common errors related to these maneuvers

Possible Outcomes of the Test

A practical test has three possible outcomes: (1) Temporary Airman Certificate (satisfactory), (2) Notice of Disapproval of Application (unsatisfactory), or (3) Letter of Discontinuance.

If the evaluator determines that a Task is incomplete, or the outcome is uncertain, the evaluator must require the applicant to repeat that Task, or portions of that Task. This provision does not mean that instruction, practice, or the repetition of an unsatisfactory Task is permitted during the practical test.

Satisfactory Performance

Refer to 14 CFR part 61, section 61.43, for satisfactory performance requirements.

Satisfactory performance will result in the issuance of a temporary certificate.

Unsatisfactory Performance

If, in the judgment of the evaluator, the applicant does not meet the standards for any Task, the applicant fails the Task and associated Area of Operation and the evaluator issues a Notice of Disapproval of Application. The evaluator lists the Area(s) of Operation in which the applicant did not meet the standard, any Area(s) of Operation not tested, and the number of practical test failures. The evaluator should also list the Tasks failed or Tasks not tested within any unsatisfactory or partially completed Area(s) of Operation. 14 CFR part 61, section 61.43(c)-(f) provides additional unsatisfactory performance requirements and parameters.

Typical areas of unsatisfactory performance and grounds for disqualification include:

- Any action or lack of action by the applicant that requires corrective intervention by the evaluator to maintain safe flight.
- Failure to use proper and effective visual scanning techniques to clear the area before and while performing maneuvers.
- Consistently exceeding tolerances stated in the skill elements of the Task.
- Failure to take prompt corrective action when tolerances are exceeded.
- Failure to exercise risk management.
- Failure to provide effective instruction while demonstrating a procedure or maneuver.

The evaluator or the applicant may end the test if the applicant fails a Task. The evaluator may continue the test only with the consent of the applicant. The applicant receives credit only for those Areas of Operation and the associated Tasks performed satisfactorily.

Letter of Discontinuance

Refer to 14 CFR part 61, section 61.43(e)(2) for conditions to issue a letter of discontinuance.

If discontinuing a practical test for reasons other than unsatisfactory performance (e.g., equipment failure, weather, illness), the evaluator must return all test paperwork to the applicant. The evaluator must prepare, sign, and issue a Letter of Discontinuance that lists those Areas of Operation the applicant successfully completed and the time period remaining to complete the test to receive credit for previously completed Areas of Operation. The evaluator should advise the applicant to present the Letter of Discontinuance to the evaluator when the practical test resumes in order to receive credit for the items successfully completed. The Letter of Discontinuance becomes part of the applicant's certification file.

Time Limit and Credit after a Discontinued Practical Test

Refer to 14 CFR part 61, sections 61.39(f) and 61.43(f) after issuance of a Letter of Discontinuance or Notice of Disapproval of Application.

Additional Rating Task Table

For an applicant who holds a Flight Instructor Certificate and seeks an additional Rotorcraft Category Helicopter Rating at the Flight Instructor level, the evaluator must evaluate that applicant in the Areas of Operation and Tasks listed in the Additional Rating Task Table. The evaluator may evaluate the applicant's competence in the remaining Areas of Operation and Tasks.

If the applicant holds two or more category or class ratings at the flight instructor level, and the ratings table indicates different Task requirements, the least restrictive entry applies. For example, if an asterisk (*) and "None" are indicated for one Area of Operation, the "None" entry applies. If the table indicates "B" and "B, C" the "B" entry applies.

Addition of a Rotorcraft Category Helicopter Rating to an Existing Flight Instructor Certificate

The table below indicates the required Tasks for each Area of Operation tested in accordance with this ACS.

Legend	
ASE	Airplane – Single-Engine
AME	Airplane – Multiengine
PL	Powered-Lift
RG	Rotorcraft – Gyroplane
G	Glider
IA	Instrument Rating – Airplane
IH	Instrument Rating – Helicopter
IP	Instrument Rating – Powered-Lift

Area of Operation	Flight Instructor Certificate and Rating(s) Held							
	ASE	AME	PL	RG	G	IA	IH	IP
I	None	None	None	None	None	None	None	None
II	*	*	*	*	*	*	*	*
III	B	B	B	B	B	*	*	*
IV	None	None	None	None	None	None	None	None
V	*	*	*	*	*	*	*	*
VI	A,C	A,C	A,C	A,C	*	*	*	*
VII	*	*	*	*	*	*	*	*
VIII	*	*	*	*	*	*	*	*
IX	*	*	*	*	*	*	*	*
X	*	*	*	*	*	*	*	*
XI	*	*	*	*	*	*	*	*
XII	*	*	*	*	*	*	*	*
XIII	*	*	*	*	*	*	*	*

Note: *An asterisk directs the evaluator to follow the selection requirements for the AOO and Tasks in the body of this ACS.*

Flight Instructor Renewal/Reinstatement

In accordance with 14 CFR part 61, section 61.199(a), the renewal or reinstatement of one rating on a Flight Instructor Certificate renews or reinstates all privileges existing on the certificate.

Renewal & Reinstatement of a Flight Instructor

Required Area of Operation	Required Tasks
I	**
II	C,L, and 1 other Task
III	1 Task
IV	1 Task
V	1 Task
VI	None
VII	1 Task
VIII	2 Takeoffs & 2 Landings
IX	None
X	1 Task
XI	2 Tasks
XII	1 Task
XIII	1 Task

Note: *A double asterisk directs the evaluator to consider the period of inactivity. The evaluator may test FOI Tasks for any reinstatement.*

Appendix 2: Safety of Flight

General

Safety of flight must be the prime consideration at all times. The evaluator, applicant, and crew must be continually alert for other traffic. If performing aspects of a given maneuver, such as emergency procedures, would jeopardize safety, the evaluator will ask the applicant to simulate that portion of the maneuver. The evaluator will assess the applicant's use of visual scanning and collision avoidance procedures throughout the entire test.

Use of Checklists

Throughout the practical test, the applicant is evaluated on the use of an appropriate checklist.

Assessing proper checklist use depends upon the specific Task. In all cases, the evaluator should determine whether the applicant demonstrates CRM, appropriately divides attention, and uses proper visual scanning. In some situations, reading the actual checklist may be impractical or unsafe. In such cases, the evaluator should assess the applicant's performance of published or recommended immediate action "memory" items along with their review of the appropriate checklist once conditions permit.

In a single-pilot aircraft, the applicant should demonstrate the crew resource management (CRM) principles described as single-pilot resource management (SRM). Proper use depends on the specific Task being evaluated. If the use of the checklist while accomplishing elements of an Objective would be either unsafe or impractical in a single-pilot operation, the applicant should review the checklist after accomplishing the elements.

Positive Exchange of Flight Controls

A clear understanding of who has control of the aircraft must exist. Prior to flight, the pilots involved should conduct a briefing that includes reviewing the procedures for exchanging flight controls.

The FAA recommends a positive three-step process for exchanging flight controls between pilots:

- When one pilot seeks to have the other pilot take control of the aircraft, they will say, "You have the flight controls."
- The second pilot acknowledges immediately by saying, "I have the flight controls."
- The first pilot again says, "You have the flight controls," and visually confirms the exchange.

Pilots should follow this procedure during any exchange of flight controls, including any occurrence during the practical test. The FAA also recommends that both pilots use a visual check to verify that the exchange has occurred. Doubt as to who is flying the aircraft should not occur.

Use of Distractions

Numerous studies indicate that many accidents have occurred when the pilot has been distracted during critical phases of flight. The evaluator should incorporate realistic distractions during the flight portion of the practical test to evaluate the pilot's situational awareness and ability to utilize proper control technique while dividing attention both inside and outside the flight deck.

Aeronautical Decision-Making, Risk Management, Crew Resource Management, and Single-Pilot Resource Management

Throughout the practical test, the evaluator must assess the applicant's ability to use sound aeronautical decision-making procedures in order to identify hazards and mitigate risk. The evaluator must accomplish this requirement by reference to the risk management elements of the given Task(s), and by developing scenarios that incorporate and combine Tasks appropriate to assessing the applicant's risk management in making safe aeronautical decisions. For example, the evaluator may develop a scenario that incorporates weather decisions and performance planning.

In assessing the applicant's performance, the evaluator should take note of the applicant's use of CRM and, if appropriate, SRM. CRM/SRM is the set of competencies that includes situational awareness, communication skills, teamwork, task allocation, and decision-making within a comprehensive framework of standard operating procedures (SOP). SRM specifically refers to the management of all resources onboard the aircraft, as well as outside resources available to the single pilot.

If an applicant fails to use aeronautical decision-making (ADM), including SRM/CRM, as applicable in any Task, the evaluator will note that Task as failed. The evaluator will also include the ADM Skill element from the Flight Deck Management Task on the Notice of Disapproval of Application.

Simulated Powerplant Failure Considerations (Single and Multiengine Helicopters)

The evaluator must conduct a pre-flight briefing that includes expectations for testing any simulated powerplant failures, to include:

- Who will initiate the simulated powerplant failure;
- The method used to simulate the powerplant failure; and
- Who will perform the power recovery procedure.

Simulated powerplant failures and autorotations must be conducted in accordance with the POH/RFM.

During a simulated powerplant failure in any helicopter, the potential for a forced landing exists. The evaluator or applicant must ensure the safety of a potential landing site before commencing any simulated powerplant failure. Such areas include, but are not limited to, hard surface runways, taxiways, and designated hard surface landing areas, such as parking lots, grass fields, and grass runways in good condition. The evaluator and applicant must also consider winds, density altitude, temperature, aircraft loading, and type of helicopter.

Minimum altitude requirements for specific Tasks are listed in Appendix 3: Aircraft, Equipment, and Operational Requirements & Limitations.

Autorotations in a Single-Engine Helicopter

Except for the Powerplant Failure in a Hover Task, if at any time during an autorotation the evaluator or the applicant determines the helicopter is not in a position to safely continue the autorotation, a power recovery and go-around must be performed. If the reason for discontinuing the autorotation is due to the applicant's lack of judgment or skill, the Task is unsatisfactory.

While an applicant's inability to complete this Task within the tolerances specified in the skill elements is considered unsatisfactory, landing area safety concerns beyond the control of the applicant or evaluator that necessitate a go-around would not be considered unsatisfactory. The applicant and evaluator must not sacrifice the safety of flight and force a landing to complete this Task.

Helicopter Touchdown Autorotation Endorsement

In lieu of testing the touchdown portion of the Tasks listed below, the evaluator has the discretion to accept a logbook endorsement from a current certificated flight instructor with a rotorcraft category and helicopter class rating who meets the requirements of 14 CFR part 61, section 61.195(h)(2). The endorsement must attest that the applicant received touchdown autorotation training and is competent in the instruction of the elements, performance, common errors, and correction of common errors related to straight-in autorotation and autorotation with turns.

- AOO X, Task B, Straight-in Autorotation in a Single-Engine Helicopter; and
- AOO X, Task C, Autorotation with Turns in a Single-Engine Helicopter

If the applicant previously received a Notice of Disapproval for either Task, the evaluator must not accept a logbook endorsement and the applicant must demonstrate touchdown autorotation(s) during the re-test. The applicant must furnish a helicopter appropriate for touchdown autorotations.

Appendix 3: Aircraft, Equipment, and Operational Requirements & Limitations

Aircraft Requirements & Limitations

If the aircraft has inoperative equipment and can be operated in accordance with 14 CFR part 91, section 91.213, it must be determined if any inoperative instruments or equipment are required to complete the practical test. The inoperative equipment must not interfere with practical test requirements.

Practical tests conducted in a flight simulation training device (FSTD) can only be accomplished as part of an approved curriculum or training program. Any limitations or powerplant failure will be noted and followed as part of that program.

Equipment Requirements & Limitations

The aircraft must meet the requirements as outlined in 14 CFR part 61, section 61.45.

To assist in management of the aircraft during the practical test, the applicant is expected to demonstrate automation management skills by utilizing installed, available, or airborne equipment such as autopilot, avionics and systems displays, and/or a flight management system (FMS). The evaluator is expected to test the applicant's knowledge of the systems that are available or installed and operative during both the ground and flight portions of the practical test. If the applicant has trained using a portable electronic flight bag (EFB) to display charts and data and wishes to use the EFB during the practical test, the applicant is expected to demonstrate appropriate knowledge, risk management, and skill appropriate to its use.

If the practical test involves maneuvering the aircraft solely by reference to instruments, the applicant is required by 14 CFR part 61, section 61.45(d)(2) to provide an appropriate view limiting device acceptable to the Administrator. The applicant and the evaluator should establish a procedure as to when and how this device should be donned and removed and brief this procedure before the flight. This device must prevent the applicant from having visual reference outside the aircraft, but it must not restrict the evaluator's ability to see and avoid other traffic. The use of the device does not apply to specific elements within a Task when there is a requirement for visual references.

Single and Multiengine Helicopters

The applicant must provide a single-engine helicopter capable of demonstrating touchdown autorotations. An applicant who brings a multiengine helicopter to the practical test must demonstrate those Task(s) specific to a multiengine helicopter in addition to all other required Tasks.

Use of Flight Simulation Training Devices (FSTD)

Applicants for a pilot certificate or rating can accomplish all or part of a practical test or proficiency check in an FSTD qualified under 14 CFR part 60, which includes full flight simulators (FFS) or flight training devices (FTD), only when conducted within an FAA-approved training program. Each operational rule part identifies additional requirements for the approval and use of FSTDs in an FAA-approved training program.

Credit for Pilot Time in an FSTD

14 CFR part 61 and part 141 specify the minimum experience requirements for each certificate or rating sought. 14 CFR part 61 and the appendices to part 141 specify the maximum amount of FFS or FTD flight training time an applicant can apply toward those experience requirements.

Use of Aviation Training Devices (ATD)

Applicants for a pilot certificate or rating cannot use an ATD to accomplish a practical test, a 14 CFR part 61, section 61.58 proficiency check, or the flight portion of a 14 CFR part 61, section 61.57 flight review. An ATD is defined in 14 CFR part 61, section 61.1.

The FAA's General Aviation and Commercial Division evaluates and approves ATDs as permitted under 14 CFR part 61, section 61.4(c) and FAA Order 8900.1. Each ATD is then issued an FAA letter of authorization (LOA) that is valid for 60 calendar months. The LOA for each ATD lists the pilot time credit allowances and associated limitations.

The Pilot Training and Certification Group public website provides a list of the FAA-approved ATDs and the associated manufacturer.

Credit for Pilot Time in an ATD

14 CFR part 61 and part 141 specify the minimum experience requirements for each certificate or rating sought. 14 CFR part 61 and the appendices to part 141 specify the maximum amount of ATD flight training time an applicant can apply toward those experience requirements. The LOA for each FAA-approved ATD lists the pilot time credit allowances and the associated limitations.

Evaluators must request an applicant to provide a copy of the manufacturer's LOA when using ATD flight training time credit to meet the minimum experience requirements for an airman pilot certificate, rating, or privilege.

Operational Requirements, Limitations, & Task Information

VII. Hovering Maneuvers

Task E. Slope Operations

Demonstration of parallel slope operations must be conducted in accordance with the helicopter manufacturer's limitations, if published. If no slope limitations are published for the helicopter being used, parallel slope operations of approximately 5-10 degrees may be demonstrated. Landings with the helicopter facing downhill or uphill will not be tested during certification. A thorough review of the intended slope operations area must be conducted to ensure clearance from hazards.

X. Performance Maneuvers

Task B. Straight-In Autorotation in a Single-Engine Helicopter

The minimum entry altitude must be a least 500 feet AGL or a suitable higher entry altitude in strong wind conditions. Initiating a go-around as a result of an applicant's inability to complete this Task within the tolerances specified in the skill elements is considered unsatisfactory. Landing area safety concerns beyond the control of the applicant or evaluator that necessitate a go-around would not be considered unsatisfactory. The applicant and evaluator must not sacrifice the safety of flight and force a landing to complete this Task.

Task C. Autorotation with Turns in a Single-Engine Helicopter

The minimum entry altitude must be above 700 feet AGL or a suitable higher entry altitude in strong wind conditions. At least two 90 degree turns in the same direction or one continuous 180-degree turn must be performed. The 180-degree turn refers to a change in direction with respect to ground track, and not an exact reciprocal heading. If the applicant does not roll out of the turn by 300 feet AGL then the evaluator must direct the applicant to perform a power recovery and initiate a go-around, and the Task is considered unsatisfactory.

XI. Emergency Operations

Task B. Powerplant Failure at Altitude in a Single-Engine Helicopter

The altitude, airspeed, and location must be considered so the helicopter is in a position to achieve a safe landing if an actual powerplant failure occurs. The minimum altitude to initiate a power failure must be at least 1,000 feet AGL with a power recovery completed by at least 500 feet AGL.

Task C. Approach and Landing with One Engine Inoperative (OEI) (simulated) (Multiengine Helicopter Only)

The evaluator must include this Task on the practical test for an applicant who provides a multiengine helicopter. The minimum altitude to initiate this Task must be at least 1000 feet AGL for this maneuver. The evaluator must conduct a preflight briefing with the applicant regarding the expectations of any simulated powerplant failure. See Appendix 2.

Task E. Recovery from Unusual Flight Attitudes

The evaluator shall conduct a preflight briefing with the applicant regarding initiation of and techniques for recovery from unusual flight attitudes. The briefing must address any hazards associated with the rotor system. Intervention by the evaluator to prevent the applicant from exceeding any helicopter operating limitations or from entering an unsafe flight condition shall be disqualifying and the Task is unsatisfactory.

Task F. Vortex Ring State (VRS)

The evaluator must conduct a briefing with the applicant regarding the selection of a safe entry altitude, recognition of the onset of VRS, and recovery within the Task standards. The area must be free of obstructions should a landing become necessary.

Task G. Low Rotor Revolutions Per Minute (RPM) Recognition and Recovery

The evaluator must test the applicant orally on this Task if the helicopter used for the practical test has a governor that cannot be disabled. During the pre-flight briefing, evaluators must discuss avoiding any condition that may lead to rotor stall during the demonstration of this Task. If the skills are tested in flight, evaluators and applicants must ensure the helicopter's main rotor system remains in a safe operating range in accordance with the POH/RFM. Evaluators must not test this Task during critical phases of flight (e.g., takeoffs or landings).

U.S. Department
of Transportation

**Federal Aviation
Administration**

FAA-G-ACS-2

Airman Certification Standards
Companion Guide for Pilots

November 2023

Flight Standards Service
Washington, DC 20591

Foreword

The Federal Aviation Administration (FAA) developed this Airman Certification Standards Companion Guide FAA-G-ACS-2, for use with the Airman Certification Standards (ACS) for pilot certification. This guide, along with the regulatory material in the ACS, may assist an applicant preparing for the knowledge and practical test(s) that lead to pilot certification. This document is intended only to provide clarity to the public regarding existing requirements under the law or agency policies. The contents of this document do not have the force and effect of law and are not meant to bind the public in any way.

This guide and the ACS are available for download from www.faa.gov.

Comments regarding this document may be emailed to acsptsinquiries@faa.gov.

Revision History

Document #	Description	Date
FAA-G-ACS-2	Airman Certification Standards Companion Guide for Pilots	November 2023

Table of Contents

Why the FAA Created this Guide

The Federal Aviation Administration (FAA) publishes the Airman Certification Standards (ACS) to communicate the aeronautical knowledge, risk management, and flight proficiency standards for various certificates and ratings available to airmen. The ACSs are incorporated by reference into 14 CFR part 61; therefore, the material contained in the ACS is regulatory. This guide, FAA-G-ACS-2, provides additional information to the regulated community to facilitate airman testing. The ACS complies with the safety management system (SMS) framework that the FAA uses to mitigate risks associated with airman certification training and testing. Specifically, the ACS, incorporated by reference (IBR) into the Federal Aviation Regulations, conforms to four functional components of an SMS:

- Safety Policy—Each ACS specifies the Tasks selected by the FAA from the regulatory Areas of Operation. Evaluators formulate a Plan of Action that determines if an applicant can operate safely within the NAS. The ACS represents the FAA's commitment to continually improve safety by including risk management elements in addition to knowledge and skill elements;

- Safety Risk Management that complies with the Administrative Procedures Act (APA) allows the FAA to work with internal and external stakeholders during document formulation. The public at large and stakeholders have an additional chance to provide input during public comment periods;

- Safety Assurance processes ensure a methodical and reasoned incorporation of changes arising from safety recommendations or new developments in aviation; and

- Safety Promotion in the form of engagement and discussion between both external stakeholders (e.g., the aviation training industry) and the FAA policy divisions going forward will determine the content of any ACS that publishes in a Notice of Proposed Rulemaking.

The FAA develops the ACS documents along with associated guidance and updated reference material in collaboration with a diverse group of aviation training experts. The goal is to drive a systematic approach to all components of the airman certification system, including knowledge test question development and conduct of the practical test. The FAA acknowledges and appreciates the many hours that these aviation experts have contributed toward this goal. This level of collaboration, a hallmark of a robust safety culture, strengthens and enhances aviation safety at every level of the airman certification system.

> **Note:** *This document does not apply to the Practical Test Standards.*

The Non-Regulatory Material in this Guide

This guide provides test preparatory information for an applicant seeking a certificate or rating. This guide also provides a list of references and abbreviations/acronyms used in any ACS and a practical test checklist for use by an applicant. The material in this guide is non-regulatory and may contain terms such as should or may:

- Should indicates actions that are recommended, but not regulatory.

- May is used in a permissive sense to state authority or permission to do the act prescribed.

This document is not legally binding and will not be relied upon by the FAA as a basis for affirmative enforcement action or other administrative penalty. Conformity with the guidance is voluntary only and nonconformity will not affect rights and obligations under existing statutes and regulations.

Section 1: Knowledge Test Eligibility, Description, and Registration

Eligibility

For detailed airman knowledge test eligibility and applicable prerequisites, applicants should refer to the 14 CFR part 61 rules that apply to a specific certificate or rating.

Steps for Knowledge Test Registration

Step 1. Obtain an FAA Tracking Number

The FAA Airman Knowledge Test registration system requires the applicant to have an FAA Tracking Number (FTN). Applicants may obtain an FTN through the Integrated Airman Certification and Rating Application (IACRA) website.

This video describes creating an IACRA account and obtaining an FTN. The specific instructions begin at the 14-minute mark.

Step 2. Create an Account with PSI

After obtaining an FTN, applicants should create an account with the FAA's contracted testing vendor, PSI, a professional testing company which operates hundreds of test centers. Visit PSI's website for information on authorized airman knowledge test centers and how to register, schedule, and pay for an Airman Knowledge Test:

> **Note:** The IACRA and PSI systems share data that verifies the applicant's FTN and name based on the information input into IACRA by the applicant. The PSI system does not allow applicants to make changes to their name. Applicants who need to make a correction to their name should process that correction in the IACRA system. The applicant's name correction will appear in the PSI system once the applicant logs back into the PSI system and refreshes their account.

Step 3. Select Test and Testing Center

After obtaining an FTN and creating an account with PSI, applicants may schedule knowledge tests. The PSI system walks the applicant through the process to select a test center in their area and select one or more specific knowledge tests.

Step 4. Select an Available Time Slot

After selecting the test center and test, the applicant may select a date and time slot.

Step 5. Pay for Test

After selecting an available time slot, the PSI system prompts the applicant to pay for the test. After completing this step, the applicant receives an automated email confirmation from PSI.

Applicants are required to meet any applicable Airman Knowledge Test eligibility requirements before arriving at a test center to take a specific knowledge test.

Testing Procedures for Applicants Requesting Special Accommodations

Applicants may request a special accommodation for their airman knowledge test through the PSI test registration and scheduling process. The process allows the applicant to select the specific accommodation(s) needed in accordance with the Americans with Disabilities Act (ADA). The PSI special accommodations team will work with the applicant and the selected testing center to provide appropriate accommodation(s). The PSI special accommodations team may request medical documentation for verification.

Acceptable Forms of Identification

14 CFR part 61, section 61.35, requires an applicant for a knowledge test to have proper identification at the time of application. Before beginning an Airman Knowledge Test, test center personnel will ask to see the applicant's state or federal government-issued photo identification. The identification must contain the applicant's photograph, signature, and date of birth. If the applicant's permanent mailing address is a PO Box number, the applicant must provide a current residential address.

Acceptable Forms of Applicant Address Verification

The table below provides examples of acceptable identification.

All Applicants	U.S. Citizens & Resident Aliens	Non-U.S. Citizens
Identification information must be: ✓ valid ✓ current Identification must include **all** of the following information: ✓ photo ✓ date of birth ✓ signature ✓ physical, residential address	✓ Identification card issued by any **U.S.** state, territory, or government entity (e.g., driver permit or license, government identification card, or military identification card) **or** ✓ Passport **or** ✓ Alien residency card	✓ Passport **and** ✓ Driver permit or license issued by a U.S. state or territory **or** ✓ Identification card issued by any government entity

Airman Knowledge Test Description

The airman knowledge test consists of multiple-choice questions. A single correct response exists for each test question. A correct response to one question does not depend upon, or influence, the correct response to another.

Taking the Knowledge Test

Before starting the actual test, the test center provides an applicant with the opportunity to practice navigating the test software. This practice or tutorial session may include sample questions to familiarize the applicant with the look and feel of the software (e.g., selecting an answer, marking a question for later review, monitoring time remaining for the test, and other features of the testing software). PSI also provides sample tests for registered users on their website.

Acceptable and Unacceptable Materials

The applicant may use the following aids, reference materials, and test materials when taking the knowledge test provided the material does not include actual test questions or answers:

Acceptable Materials	Unacceptable Materials	Notes
Supplement book provided by the proctor	Written materials that are handwritten, printed, or electronic	Testing centers may provide calculators and/or deny the use of personal calculators.
All models of aviation-oriented calculators or small electronic calculators that perform only arithmetic functions	Electronic calculators incorporating permanent or continuous type memory circuits without erasure capability	Proctor may prohibit the use of an applicant's calculator if the proctor is unable to determine the calculator's erasure capability
Calculators with simple programmable memories, which allow the addition to, subtraction from, or retrieval of one number from the memory, or simple functions, such as square root and percentages	Magnetic Cards, magnetic tapes, modules, computer chips, or any other device upon which pre-written programs or information related to the test can be stored and retrieved	Printouts of data should be surrendered at the completion of the test if the calculator incorporates this design feature
Scales, straightedges, protractors, plotters, navigation computers, blank log sheets, holding pattern entry aids, and electronic or mechanical calculators that are directly related to the test	Dictionaries	Before, and upon completion of the test, while in the presence of the proctor, actuate the ON/OFF switch or RESET button, and perform any other function that ensures erasure of any data stored in memory circuits
Manufacturer's permanently inscribed instructions on the front and back of such aids (e.g., formulas, conversions, regulations, signals, weather data, holding pattern diagrams, frequencies, weight and balance formulas, and air traffic control procedures)	Any booklet or manual containing instructions related to the use of test aids	Proctor makes the final determination regarding aids, reference materials, and test materials

Test Taking Tips

When taking a knowledge test, applicants should:
- Read the test instructions carefully;
- Mark difficult questions for later review in order to use the available time efficiently;
- Examine graphs and notes that pertain to the question;
- Request and mark a printed copy of any graph while computing answers, if needed;
- Understand that since only one answer is complete and correct, the other possible answers are either incomplete or erroneous;
- Answer each question in accordance with the current regulations and guidance publications; and
- Answer all the questions before time allotted for the test expires.
- Review 14 CFR part 61, section 61.37 regarding cheating or other unauthorized conduct.

Section 2: Airman Knowledge Test Report

Upon completion of the knowledge test, the test center issues a printed Airman Knowledge Test Report (AKTR) to the applicant, which documents the applicant's test score and lists a code for any questions answered incorrectly. The applicant should retain the original AKTR. During the oral portion of a practical test, the evaluator reviews the AKTR, and assesses any noted areas of deficiency.

Applicant Name Considerations for the Airman Knowledge Test Report and the Practical Test

The FAA compares the applicant's name on the AKTR with the name on the practical test application form when examining certificate and rating applications and before issuing a permanent certificate to the applicant. If an incorrect middle initial, spelling variant, or different middle name is on the AKTR or if there is a first name variation of any kind between the AKTR and the formal application for a certificate or rating, the evaluator for the practical test should attach an explanation and a copy of the applicant's photo identification to the IACRA or paper application. An IACRA application cannot be processed if the applicant's last name or suffix (e.g., Jr., Sr.) on the AKTR does not match the name recorded on the application form. In this case, the applicant should use a paper application, and the evaluator should include an explanation and copy of the applicant's photo identification to avoid a correction notice.

Retesting After Failure of AKTR

An applicant retesting after the failure of any Airman Knowledge Test may retest with appropriate authorization. The applicant should bring the applicable AKTR indicating failure to the test center, along with an endorsement from an Authorized Instructor who gave the applicant the required additional training in accordance with 14 CFR part 61, section 61.49. The endorsement certifies that the applicant is competent to pass the knowledge test.

Knowledge Test Codes During Transition from PTS To ACS

When a PTS is the effective standard for a specific certificate or rating, the applicant receives an Airman Knowledge Test Report with pilot (PLT) codes that correspond to any knowledge test question(s) the applicant answered incorrectly. For example: PLT044.

For knowledge tests taken after an ACS becomes the effective standard for a specific certificate or rating, the test center issues an AKTR with ACS codes that correspond to any knowledge test question(s) the applicant answered incorrectly. For example: CA.I.A.K1

During a period of transition after an ACS replaces a PTS, an applicant could possess a valid AKTR with PLT codes. When this occurs, instructors and evaluators can continue to use PLT codes in conjunction with the appropriate ACS for targeting training and retesting of missed knowledge subject areas by looking up the PLT code(s) in the Learning Statement Reference Guide.

After noting the subject area(s) for the PLT codes, instructors and evaluators should check or test the applicant's understanding of that material in the context of the appropriate ACS Area(s) of Operation and Task(s).

> *Note:* *Test codes for the Fundamentals of Instructing knowledge test are the same for all instructor certificates and will issue with ACS codes after the first instructor ACS becomes effective.*

ACS Archived Test Codes

As a result of updates made to an ACS, an AKTR may contain one or more archived ACS codes. These codes are indicated as archived within the ACS. For example:

> PA.VIII.E.K1a   Archived.

Use of archived codes in the ACS avoids code shifting that could create ambiguity when looking up ACS codes listed on an AKTR. An unexpired AKTR may span ACS revisions and ACS codes may archive after an applicant takes a knowledge test. Therefore, an applicant, instructor, or evaluator may need to interpret one or more archived ACS codes on an AKTR. Individuals can refer to the ACS revision in effect on the date of the knowledge test or to section 8 of this guide for archived ACS codes and the associated element text.

Use of archived codes in the ACS avoids code shifting that could create ambiguity when looking up ACS codes listed on an AKTR. An unexpired AKTR may span ACS revisions and ACS codes may archive after an applicant takes a knowledge test. Therefore, an applicant, instructor, or evaluator may need to interpret one or more archived ACS codes on an AKTR. Individuals can refer to the ACS revision in effect on the date of the knowledge test or to Section 8 of this guide for archived ACS codes and the associated element text. For example, the archived ACS code for Private Pilot Airplane element PA.VIII.E.K1a is noted in Section 8 of this guide as: Sensitivity, limitations, and potential errors in unusual attitudes.

Obtaining a Duplicate AKTR

If the applicant's knowledge test was taken on or after January 13, 2020, the applicant can print a duplicate or expired test report (AKTR) by visiting the PSI website.

If the knowledge test was taken on or before January 10, 2020, the applicant should follow 14 CFR, section 61.29 for replacement of a lost or destroyed AKTR.

Section 3: ACS Risk Management

Risk management involves perception of hazards, the ability to process the probability and severity of outcomes associated with any hazard, and performance of appropriate risk mitigation as needed to preserve the desired margin of safety.

Previous editions of the ACS often used elements for evaluation of risk management as encompassing a failure to do something. Many of these "failure to act" elements mimicked skill elements and limited an evaluator's opportunity to thoroughly examine an applicant's understanding of risk management.

For example, see elements R1 and S2 from the Private Pilot — Airplane Airman Certification Standards (FAA-S-ACS-6B with Change 1) in the excerpt below:

Task	C. Systems and Equipment Malfunctions
References	FAA-H-8083-2, FAA-H-8083-3; POH/AFM
Objective	To determine that the applicant exhibits satisfactory knowledge, risk management, and skills associated with system and equipment malfunctions appropriate to the airplane provided for the practical test and analyzing the situation and take appropriate action for simulated emergencies.
Knowledge	The applicant demonstrates understanding of:
PA.IX.C.K1	Partial or complete power loss related to the specific powerplant, including:
PA.IX.C.K1a	a. Engine roughness or overheat
PA.IX.C.K1b	b. Carburetor or induction icing
PA.IX.C.K1c	c. Loss of oil pressure
PA.IX.C.K1d	d. Fuel starvation
PA.IX.C.K2	System and equipment malfunctions specific to the airplane, including:
PA.IX.C.K2a	a. Electrical malfunction
PA.IX.C.K2b	b. Vacuum/pressure and associated flight instrument malfunctions
PA.IX.C.K2c	c. Pitot/static system malfunction
PA.IX.C.K2d	d. Electronic flight deck display malfunction
PA.IX.C.K2e	e. Landing gear or flap malfunction
PA.IX.C.K2f	f. Inoperative trim
PA.IX.C.K3	Smoke/fire/engine compartment fire.
PA.IX.C.K4	Any other system specific to the airplane (e.g., supplemental oxygen, deicing).
PA.IX.C.K5	Inadvertent door or window opening.
Risk Management	The applicant demonstrates the ability to identify, assess and mitigate risks, encompassing:
PA.IX.C.R1	Failure to use the proper checklist for a system or equipment malfunction.
PA.IX.C.R2	Distractions, loss of situational awareness, or improper task management.
Skills	The applicant demonstrates the ability to:
PA.IX.C.S1	Describe appropriate action for simulated emergencies specified by the evaluator, from at least three of the elements or sub-elements listed in K1 through K5 above.
PA.IX.C.S2	Complete the appropriate checklist.

The FAA reworded risk elements that describe a Failure to... (or similar phrases) with language permitting an open-ended examination of risk management by the evaluator. See element R2 in the excerpt below (image for illustration purposes only):

Task C. Systems and Equipment Malfunctions

References: *FAA-H-8083-2, FAA-H-8083-3, FAA-H-8083-25; POH/AFM*

Objective: To determine the applicant exhibits satisfactory knowledge, risk management, and skills associated with system and equipment malfunctions appropriate to the airplane provided for the practical test.

Knowledge:	The applicant demonstrates understanding of:
PA.IX.C.K1	Causes of partial or complete power loss related to the specific type of powerplant(s).
PA.IX.C.K1a	a. [Archived]
PA.IX.C.K1b	b. [Archived]
PA.IX.C.K1c	c. [Archived]
PA.IX.C.K1d	d. [Archived]
PA.IX.C.K2	System and equipment malfunctions specific to the aircraft, including:
PA.IX.C.K2a	a. Electrical malfunction
PA.IX.C.K2b	b. Vacuum/pressure and associated flight instrument malfunctions
PA.IX.C.K2c	c. Pitot-static system malfunction
PA.IX.C.K2d	d. Electronic flight deck display malfunction
PA.IX.C.K2e	e. Landing gear or flap malfunction
PA.IX.C.K2f	f. Inoperative trim
PA.IX.C.K3	Causes and remedies for smoke or fire onboard the aircraft.
PA.IX.C.K4	Any other system specific to the aircraft (e.g., supplemental oxygen, deicing).
PA.IX.C.K5	Inadvertent door or window opening.

Risk Management:	The applicant is able to identify, assess, and mitigate risk associated with:
PA.IX.C.R1	Checklist usage for a system or equipment malfunction.
PA.IX.C.R2	Distractions, task prioritization, loss of situational awareness, or disorientation.
PA.IX.C.R3	Undesired aircraft state.
PA.IX.C.R4	Startle response.

Skills:	The applicant exhibits the skill to:
PA.IX.C.S1	Determine appropriate action for simulated emergencies specified by the evaluator, from at least three of the elements or sub-elements listed in K1 through K5.
PA.IX.C.S2	Complete the appropriate checklist(s).

Section 4: Flight Instructor Applicant Considerations

Flight Instructor ACS Information

Flight Instructor ACS documents include sections that define the acceptable standards for knowledge, risk management, and skills unique to an instructor certificate or rating.

Knowledge elements often begin with "The applicant demonstrates instructional knowledge by describing and explaining…" Instructional knowledge means the instructor applicant can effectively present the what, how, and why involved with the task elements using techniques described in the fundamentals of instructing (FOI) area of operation in an instructor ACS.

The Fundamentals of Instructing (FOI), Area of Operation I, Task F: Elements of Effective Teaching that include Risk Management and Accident Prevention focuses on teaching risk management and on those risks encountered by a flight instructor while providing in-flight instruction.

Instructor applicants deal with additional risk management on several levels. These include teaching risk management in the classroom and mitigation of risk during flight instruction.

Note that the FOI sections in each instructor ACS are identical and use the same element codes. This makes it possible to use the same FOI elements for every instructor ACS.

Section 5: References

The ACS are based on the following 14 CFR parts, FAA guidance documents, manufacturer's publications, and other documents.

Note: *Users should reference the current edition of the reference documents listed below. The current edition of all FAA publications can be found at www.faa.gov.*

Reference	Title
14 CFR part 1	Definitions and Abbreviations
14 CFR part 23	Airworthiness Standards: Normal Category Airplanes
14 CFR part 25	Airworthiness Standards: Transport Category Airplanes
14 CFR part 27	Airworthiness Standards: Normal Category Rotorcraft
14 CFR part 29	Airworthiness Standards: Transport Category Rotorcraft
14 CFR part 39	Airworthiness Directives
14 CFR part 43	Maintenance, Preventive Maintenance, Rebuilding, and Alteration
14 CFR part 61	Certification: Pilots, Flight Instructors, and Ground Instructors
14 CFR part 63	Certification: Flight Crewmembers other than Pilots
14 CFR part 65	Certification: Airmen Other Than Flightcrew Members
14 CFR part 67	Medical Standards and Certification
14 CFR part 68	Requirements for Operating Certain Small Aircraft Without a Medical Certificate
14 CFR part 71	Designation of Class A, B, C, D, and E Airspace Areas; Air Traffic Service Routes; and Reporting Points
14 CFR part 91	General Operating and Flight Rules
14 CFR part 93	Special Air Traffic Rules
14 CFR part 97	Standard Instrument Procedures
14 CFR part 117	Flight and Duty Limitations and Rest Requirements: Flightcrew Members
14 CFR part 119	Certification: Air Carriers and Commercial Operators
14 CFR part 121	Operating Requirements: Domestic, Flag, and Supplemental Operations
14 CFR part 135	Operating Requirements: Commuter and on Demand Operations and Rules Governing Persons on Board Such Aircraft
49 CFR part 830	Notification and Reporting of Aircraft Accidents or Incidents and Overdue Aircraft, and Preservation of Aircraft Wreckage, Mail, Cargo, and Records
AC 00-30	Clear Air Turbulence Avoidance
AC 00-46	Aviation Safety Reporting Program
AC 20-117	Hazards Following Ground Deicing and Ground Operations in Conditions Conducive to Aircraft Icing
AC 29-2	Certification of Transport Category Rotorcraft
AC 60-22	Aeronautical Decision Making
AC 60-28	FAA English Language Standard for an FAA Certificate Issued Under 14 CFR Parts 61, 63, 65, and 107
AC 61-65	Certification: Pilots and Flight and Ground Instructors

Reference	Title
AC 61-67	Stall and Spin Awareness Training
AC 61-107	Aircraft Operations at Altitudes Above 25,000 Feet Mean Sea Level or Mach Numbers Greater Than .75
AC 61-138	Airline Transport Pilot Certification Training Program
AC 61-140	Autorotation Training
AC 68-1	BasicMed
AC 90-48	Pilots' Role in Collision Avoidance
AC 90-95	Unanticipated Right Yaw in Helicopters
AC 90-100	U.S Terminal and En Route Area Navigation (RNAV) Operations
AC 90-105	Approval Guidance for RNP Operations and Barometric Vertical Navigation in the U.S. National Airspace System and in Oceanic and Remote Continental Airspace
AC 90-107	Guidance for Localizer Performance with Vertical Guidance and Localizer Performance without Vertical Guidance Approach Operations in the U.S. National Airspace System
AC 90-117	Data Link Communications
AC 91.21-1	Use of Portable Electronic Devices Aboard Aircraft
AC 91-32	Safety in and Around Helicopters
AC 91-55	Reduction of Electrical System Failures Following Aircraft Engine Starting
AC 91-73	Parts 91 and 135 Single Pilot, Flight School Procedures During Taxi Operations
AC 91-74	Pilot Guide: Flight in Icing Conditions
AC 91-78	Use of Class 1 or Class 2 Electronic Flight Bag (EFB)
AC 91-79	Mitigating the Risks of a Runway Overrun Upon Landing
AC 91-92	Pilot's Guide to a Preflight Briefing
AC 120-27	Aircraft Weight and Balance Control
AC 120-51	Crew Resource Management Training
AC 120-57	Surface Movement Guidance and Control System
AC 120-58	Pilot Guide Large Aircraft Ground Deicing
AC 120-60	Ground Deicing and Anti-icing Program
AC 120-66	Aviation Safety Action Program (ASAP)
AC 120-71	Standard Operating Procedures and Pilot Monitoring Duties for Flight Deck Crewmembers
AC 120-74	Parts 91, 121, 125, and 135 Flightcrew Procedures During Taxi Operations
AC 120-76	Authorization for Use of Electronic Flight Bags
AC 120-82	Flight Operational Quality Assurance (FOQA)
AC 120-90	Line Operations Safety Audit (LOSA)
AC 120-100	Basics of Aviation Fatigue
AC 120-101	Part 121 Air Carrier Operational Control
AC 120-108	Continuous Descent Final Approach

Reference	Title
AC 120-109	Stall Prevention and Recovery Training
AC 120-111	Upset Prevention and Recovery Training
AC 135-17	Pilot Guide - Small Aircraft Ground Deicing
AFM	Airplane Flight Manual
AIM	Aeronautical Information Manual
AC 120-100	Basics of Aviation Fatigue
AC 120-101	Part 121 Air Carrier Operational Control
AC 120-108	Continuous Descent Final Approach
AC 120-109	Stall Prevention and Recovery Training
AC 120-111	Upset Prevention and Recovery Training
AC 135-17	Pilot Guide - Small Aircraft Ground Deicing
AFM	Airplane Flight Manual
AIM	Aeronautical Information Manual
Applicable Manufacturer's Equipment Supplement(s)	Manufacturer's Equipment Supplement(s)
Appropriate Manufacturer's Safety Notices	Safety Notices
Chart Supplements	Chart Supplements
Digital-Visual Charts (d-VC)	Digital-Visual Charts (d-VC)
FAA-H-8083-1	Aircraft Weight and Balance Handbook
FAA-H-8083-2	Risk Management Handbook
FAA-H-8083-3	Airplane Flying Handbook
FAA-H-8083-9	Aviation Instructor's Handbook
FAA-H-8083-15	Instrument Flying Handbook
FAA-H-8083-16	Instrument Procedures Handbook
FAA-H-8083-21	Helicopter Flying Handbook
FAA-H-8083-23	Seaplane, Skiplane, and Float/Ski Equipped Helicopter Operations Handbook
FAA-H-8083-25	Pilot's Handbook of Aeronautical Knowledge
FAA-H-8083-28	Aviation Weather Handbook
FAA Order 8130.2	Airworthiness Certification of Aircraft
FAA-P-8740-66	Flying Light Twins Safely
FSB Report (type specific)	Flight Standardization Board Report (if available)
Helicopter Route Charts	Helicopter Route Charts
IFR Enroute Charts	IFR Enroute Low Altitude and IFR Enroute High Altitude Charts
NOTAMs	Notices to Air Missions
PDC	Profile Descent Charts

Reference	Title
POH/AFM	Pilot's Operating Handbook/FAA-Approved Airplane Flight Manual
POH/Flight Manual	Pilot's Operating Handbook/FAA-Approved Flight Manual
POH/RFM	Pilot's Operating Handbook/FAA-Approved Rotorcraft Flight Manual
QRH	Quick Reference Handbook
SAFO 16016	Helicopter Stabilized Hover Checks Before Departure
SAFO 17010	Incorrect Airport Surface Approaches and Landings
SAFO 19001	Landing Performance Assessments at Time of Arrival
STARs	Standard Terminal Arrival Routes
TPP	Terminal Procedures Publications
USCG Navigation Rules	USCG Navigation Rules, International-Inland
VFR Navigation Charts	Sectional/Terminal Aeronautical Charts

Section 6: Abbreviations and Acronyms

Note: *Users should reference the current edition of the reference documents listed below. The current edition of all FAA publications can be found at www.faa.gov.*

Acronym	Description
14 CFR	Title 14 of the Code of Federal Regulations
AATD	Advanced Aviation Training Device
AC	Advisory Circular
ACS	Airman Certification Standards
ADM	Aeronautical Decision-Making
ADS-B	Automatic Dependent Surveillance Broadcast
ADS-C	Automatic Dependent Surveillance - Contract
AFCS	Automatic Flight Control System
AFM	Airplane Flight Manual
AGL	Above Ground Level
AIM	Aeronautical Information Manual
AIRMET	Airman's Meteorological Information
AKTR	Airman Knowledge Test Report
AMEL	Airplane Multiengine Land
AMES	Airplane Multiengine Sea
APU	Auxiliary Power Unit
ASEL	Airplane Single-Engine Land
ASES	Airplane Single-Engine Sea
ASI	Aviation Safety Inspector
ATC	Air Traffic Control
ATD	Aviation Training Device
ATP	Airline Transport Pilot
BATD	Basic Aviation Training Device
CDI	Course Deviation Indicator
CDL	Configuration Deviation List
CFIT	Controlled Flight Into Terrain
CFR	Code of Federal Regulations
CG	Center of Gravity
CPDLC	Controller–pilot data link communication
CRM	Crew Resource Management
DA	Decision Altitude
DDA	Derived Decision Altitude

Acronym	Description
DH	Decision Height
DME	Distance Measuring Equipment
DP	Departure Procedures
EFB	Electronic Flight Bag
EFC	Expect Further Clearance
EFIS	Electronic Flight Instrument System
ELT	Emergency Locator Transmitter
ETA	Estimated Time of Arrival
ETL	Effective Translational Lift
FAA	Federal Aviation Administration
FAF	Final Approach Fix
FB	Wind and Temperature Aloft Forecast
FFS	Full Flight Simulator
FMS	Flight Management System
FRAT	Flight Risk Assessment Tool
FSB	Flight Standardization Board
FSO	Flight Standards Office
FSTD	Flight Simulation Training Device
FTD	Flight Training Device
G	Unit of Force Equal to Earth's Gravity
GBAS	Ground Based Augmentation System
GFA	Graphical Forecast for Aviation
GNSS	Global Navigation Satellite System
GPS	Global Positioning System
H/V	Height/Velocity
HF	High Frequency
HIGE	Hover in Ground Effect
HUD	Head Up Display
IFR	Instrument Flight Rules
ILS	Instrument Landing System
IMC	Instrument Meteorological Conditions
INFO	Information for Operators
INS	Inertial Navigation System
IOS	Instructor Operating Station
KOEL	Kinds of Operations Equipment List
L/DMAX	Lift/Drag Maximum

Acronym	Description
LAHSO	Land and Hold Short Operations
LNAV	Lateral Navigation
LOA	Letter of Authorization
LOC-I	Loss of Control in Flight
LP	Localizer Performance
LTE	Loss of Tail Rotor Effectiveness
LTM	Long Term Memory
MAP	Missed Approach Point
MDA	Minimum Descent Altitude
MEL	Minimum Equipment List
METAR	Aviation Routine Weather Reports (Meteorological Aerodrome Report)
MFD	Multi-Function Display
MMO	Maximum Operating Limit Speed as a Mach Number
NAS	National Airspace System
NOTAM	Notice to Air Missions
Nr	Main Rotor Speed
NSP	National Simulator Program
NTSB	National Transportation Safety Board
ODP	Obstacle Departure Procedure
OEI	One Engine Inoperative
PAVE	Risk Management Checklist for Pilot/Aircraft/enVironment/External Factors
PFD	Primary Flight Display
PIC	Pilot-in-Command
PinS	Copter Point in Space
PIREP	Pilot Report
POA	Plan of Action
POH	Pilot's Operating Handbook
PTS	Practical Test Standards
QPS	Qualification Performance Standard
QRH	Quick Reference Handbook
RAIM	Receiver Autonomous Integrity Monitoring
RCAM	Runway Condition Assessment Matrix
RFM	Rotorcraft Flight Manual
RNAV	Area Navigation
RNP	Required Navigation Performance
RPM	Revolutions Per Minute

Acronym	Description
SAE	Specialty Aircraft Examiner
SAFO	Safety Alert for Operators
SATR	Special Air Traffic Rules
SBAS	Satellite Based Augmentation System
SBT	Scenario Based Training
SFAR	Special Federal Aviation Regulation
SFRA	Special Flight Rules Area
SID	Standard Instrument Departure
SIGMET	Significant Meteorological Information
SMS	Safety Management System
SRM	Single-Pilot Resource Management
SRM	Safety Risk Management
STAR	Standard Terminal Arrival
STM	Short Term Memory
SUA	Special Use Airspace
TAF	Terminal Area Forecast
TAWS	Terrain Awareness and Warning System
TCAS	Traffic Collision Avoidance System
TCDS	Type Certificate Data Sheet
TCE	Training Center Evaluator
TEM	Threat and Error Management
TFR	Temporary Flight Restrictions
TPP	Terminal Procedures Publication
TUC	Time of Useful Consciousness
UHF	Ultra High Frequency
UIMC	Unintended Instrument Meteorological Conditions
USCG	United States Coast Guard
UTC	Coordinated Universal Time
V_1	The maximum speed in the takeoff at which the pilot must take the first action (e.g., apply brakes, reduce thrust, deploy speed brakes) to stop the airplane within the accelerate-stop distance. V_1 also means the minimum speed in the takeoff, following a failure of the critical engine at V_{EF}, at which the pilot can continue the takeoff and achieve the required height above the takeoff surface within the takeoff distance.
V_2	Takeoff Safety Speed
V_A	Maneuvering speed
VDP	Visual Descent Point
VFR	Visual Flight Rules

Acronym	Description
V_{MC}	Minimum control speed with the critical engine inoperative
VHF	Very High Frequency
VMC	Visual Meteorological Conditions
V_{MCG}	Minimum control speed on the ground with the critical engine inoperative
V_{MO}	Maximum Operating Limit Speed
V_{NE}	Never exceed speed
VCOA	Visual Climb Over Airport
VOR	Very High Frequency Omnidirectional Range
V_R	Rotation speed
V_{REF}	Reference Landing Speed
VRS	Vortex Ring State
V_S	Stall Speed
V_{SO}	Stalling Speed or the Minimum Steady Flight Speed in the Landing Configuration
V_{SSE}	Safe, intentional one-engine-inoperative speed. Originally known as safe single-engine speed
VTOL	Vertical Takeoff and Landing
V_X	Best angle of climb airspeed
V_{XSE}	Best angle of climb speed with one engine inoperative
V_Y	Best rate of climb speed
V_{YSE}	Best rate of climb speed with one engine inoperative.
WAAS	Wide Area Augmentation System

Section 7: Practical Test Checklist (Applicant)

Evaluator's Name: _____

Location: _____

Date/Time: _____

Acceptable Aircraft

☐ Aircraft Documents:

    ☐ Airworthiness Certificate

    ☐ Registration Certificate

    ☐ Operating Limitations

☐ Aircraft Maintenance Records:

    ☐ Logbook Record of Airworthiness Inspections and Airworthiness Directives (AD) Compliance

☐ Pilot's Operating Handbook and FAA-Approved Aircraft Flight Manual

Personal Equipment

☐ View-Limiting Device

☐ Current Aeronautical Charts (printed or electronic)

☐ Computer and Plotter

☐ Flight Plan Form and Flight Logs (printed or electronic)

☐ Chart Supplements, Airport Diagrams, and Appropriate Publications (printed or electronic)

☐ Current AIM (printed or electronic)

Personal Records

☐ Government-Issued Identification—Photo/Signature Identification (ID)

☐ Pilot Certificate

☐ Current Medical Certificate or BasicMed Qualification (when applicable)

☐ Completed FAA Form 8710-1, Airman Certificate and/or Rating Application, or completed IACRA form, FAA Form 8710-11, Airman Certificate and/or Rating Application—Sport Pilot, or FAA Form 8400.3, Airman Certificate and/or Rating Application with Instructor's Signature, if applicable

☐ Airman Knowledge Test Report

☐ Airman's Logbook with Appropriate Instructor Endorsements

☐ FAA Form 8060-5, Notice of Disapproval (if applicable)

☐ Letter of Discontinuance (if applicable)

☐ Approved School Graduation Certificate (if applicable)

Section 8: Knowledge Test Reports and Archived ACS Codes

Private Pilot for Airplane Category ACS Archived Codes

PA.III.A.R3   Confirmation or expectation bias.

PA.IV.A.S10   Retract the water rudders, as appropriate, establish and maintain the most efficient planing/liftoff attitude, and correct for porpoising and skipping (ASES, AMES).

PA.IV.I.S5   Retract the water rudders as appropriate; advance the throttle smoothly to takeoff power.

PA.IV.K.S7   Retract the water rudders as appropriate; advance the throttle smoothly to takeoff power.

PA.VIII.E.K1a   Sensitivity, limitations, and potential errors in unusual attitudes

PA.VIII.E.K1b   Correlation (pitch instruments/bank instruments)

PA.VIII.E.K1c   Function and operation

PA.VIII.E.K1d   Proper instrument cross-check techniques

PA.VIII.E.R2   Failure to seek assistance or declare an emergency in a deteriorating situation.

PA.VIII.E.R6   Failure to unload the wings in recovering from high G situations.

PA.VIII.F.S3   Maintain altitude ±200 feet, heading ±20°, and airspeed ±10 knots.

PA.IX.C.K1a   Maintain altitude ±200 feet, heading ±20°, and airspeed ±10 knots

PA.IX.C.K1b   Engine roughness or overheat

PA.IX.C.K1c   Loss of oil pressure

PA.IX.C.K1d   Fuel starvation

PA.XII.A.R2   Confirmation or expectation bias as related to taxi instructions.

PA.XII.A.S1   Demonstrate runway incursion avoidance procedures.

PA.XII.B.R2   Confirmation or expectation bias as related to taxi instructions.

Commercial Pilot for Airplane Category ACS Archived Codes

CA.I.F.K2f   Weight and balance

CA.IV.A.S10   Retract the water rudders, as appropriate, establish and maintain the most efficient planing/liftoff attitude, and correct for porpoising and skipping (ASES, AMES).

CA.IV.I.S5   Retract the water rudders as appropriate; advance the throttle smoothly to takeoff power.

CA.IV.K.S7   Retract the water rudders as appropriate; advance the throttle smoothly to takeoff power.

CA.IV.B.S5   Recognize signal loss or interference and take appropriate action, if applicable.

CA.IX.C.K1a   Engine roughness or overheat

CA.IX.C.K1b   Carburetor or induction icing

CA.IX.C.K1c   Loss of oil pressure

CA.IX.C.K1d   Fuel starvation

CA.XI.A.R2   Confirmation or expectation bias as related to taxi instructions.

CA.XI.A.S1   Utilize runway incursion avoidance procedures.

CA.XI.B.R2   Confirmation or expectation bias as related to taxi instructions.

Instrument Rating – Airplane ACS Archived Codes

IR.IV.B.R2   Failure to recognize an unusual flight attitude and follow the proper recovery procedure.

IR.VII.C.R2   Collision hazards, to include aircraft, terrain, obstacles, wires, vehicles, vessels, persons, and wildlife.

Airline Transport Pilot and Type Rating ACS Archived Codes

AA.IV.B.R2   Failure to recognize an unusual flight attitude and follow the proper recovery procedure.

AA.V.A.S2   When accomplished in an FSTD, the entry should be consistent with the expected operational environment for a stall on takeoff or while on approach in a partial flap configuration with no minimum entry altitude defined.

AA.V.B.S2   When accomplished in an FSTD, the entry should be consistent with the expected operational environment for a stall in cruise flight with no minimum entry altitude defined.

AA.V.C.S2   When accomplished in an FSTD, the entry should be consistent with the expected operational environment for a stall when fully configured for landing with no minimum entry altitude defined.

AA.VI.F.R3   Planning for.

AA.VI.F.R3a   a. Missed Approach

AA.VI.F.R3b   b. Land and hold short operations (LAHSO)

AA.VI.H.R3   Planning for.

AA.VI.H.R3a   a. Missed Approach

AA.VI.H.R3b   b. Land and hold short operations (LAHSO)

AA.VIII.A.R2   Confirmation or expectation bias as related to taxi instructions.

AA.VIII.B.R2   Confirmation or expectation bias as related to taxi instructions.

U.S. Department of Transportation
Federal Aviation Administration

FAA-S-ACS-29
Includes FAA-G-ACS-2

Airman Certification Standards

Flight Instructor

Helicopter

Flight Standards Service
Washington, DC 20591

Aviation Supplies & Academics, Inc.
Newcastle, Washington 98059